A Leader's Guide to

I Like Being ME

Poems for Children About Feeling Special, Appreciating Others, and Getting Along

By
Judy Lalli, M.S.
and Mary Martha Whitworth, M.A.

Free Spirit® PUBLISHING

Edited by Marjorie Lisovskis
Supervising editor: Pamela Espeland
Cover design by Ann Elliot Artz
Interior design and production by City Desktop Productions., Inc.
Author photographs by John Kellar Photography, Skippack, Pennsylvania

10 9 8 7 6 5 4 3 2 1

Free Spirit Publishing Inc.
400 First Avenue North, Suite 616
Minneapolis, Minnesota 55401-1730
(612) 338-2068
help4kids@freespirit.com

Dedication

To my loving parents, Russ and Fagel Goldsmith
J.L.

To my very special children, Liesl, Peter, and Toryn
M.M.W.

Acknowledgments

We want to thank the many wonderful teachers who have shared their ideas with us over the years. They have inspired us with their enthusiasm, creativity, and dedication to children.

We also wish to thank our outstanding editor, Margie Lisovskis, who has consistently challenged us, listened to us, and supported us. Her contributions to this project enriched both the process and the final product.

Contents

List of Reproducible Pages

Introduction

Every child is special, and every child deserves to know this. Children need to value themselves and others, appreciate the qualities that make each person unique, and do their best to live in harmony with other children and adults. They need to recognize that they, personally, can *decide* to do these things.

This book was written as a companion guide to *I Like Being Me: Poems for Children About Feeling Special, Appreciating Others, and Getting Along* by Judy Lalli. Together with the poetry book, the activities in this Leader's Guide provide an introduction to self-esteem and empowerment for young children based on these beliefs:

- Children can learn to value what is unique in themselves and others.
- Children can learn to understand and express their feelings.
- Children can learn to make decisions and take responsibility for their actions.
- Children can learn from their mistakes.
- Children can learn to cooperate and resolve conflicts peacefully.

The poems and photographs in *I Like Being Me* and the activities in this Leader's Guide are truly "child-tested." Many children eagerly and enthusiastically tried out different versions of the poems and, in doing so, helped adjust the language and rhythms. Teaching colleagues and students alike helped us shape and refine each activity.

How to Use This Book

You can use the lessons in *A Leader's Guide to I Like Being Me* with children in preschool, kindergarten, elementary school, day care, religious school, youth groups, counseling groups, homes, or other settings. The poems and accompanying photographs in the children's book have an immediate appeal. Children enjoy hearing, learning, reciting, role-playing, discussing, and remembering the poems. The activities in this Leader's Guide reinforce and expand on the character-building themes represented by the poems and pictures. Through reading, listening, questioning, moving, creating, thinking, speaking, sharing, writing, and collaborating, children learn that they have the power to make personal choices, work together, and solve problems.

A Leader's Guide to I Like Being Me includes 26 lessons. Each lesson focuses on a different theme (such as believing in myself, learning from mistakes, understanding others, cooperating, and celebrating differences), which is introduced by a poem. Every lesson includes one or two activities designed to reinforce and enhance the theme. Most activities take 15–20 minutes and require a minimum of preparation. The lessons provide a mix of individual, small-group, and large-group experiences that help children explore the themes through a variety of learning styles and modes.

Before beginning the lessons, read the poems in *I Like Being Me* and look at the accompanying photographs. Then look through the table of contents in this Leader's Guide to see the theme each poem addresses. Decide what order you want to follow in presenting the lessons. One approach is to use them sequentially. To do this, we recommend that you introduce a new theme each week. Write the theme on the board and refer to it throughout the week as you use the poem and lesson. There is a progression from those themes dealing with *myself* (having a positive attitude, liking myself, speaking up for myself) to those involving interactions with *others* (telling the truth, being a friend, getting along). If you choose to teach the lessons consecutively, the themes will build on and complement one another.

As an alternative, you may choose to teach the lessons in a different sequence. The themes are independent and may be presented in any order. This Leader's Guide is designed so you can easily turn to a lesson "on the spot" to address a specific situation. For example, you may want to correlate the lessons with language arts, social studies, or health units. Throughout the year, you can return to themes and lessons as their message relates to what's going on in your group.

How to Begin

On page 3, you'll find a letter to parents and caregivers that announces and introduces the program. Send a copy of the letter home with the children in your group when you begin using the *I Like Being Me* poems and lessons.

The children's book presents 26 poems and accompanying photographs. Each poem introduces a lesson theme. You can begin each lesson by sharing the poem with your students, encouraging them to recite it, and discussing what it means. Before presenting a poem, you might find it helpful to practice it until you've found a comfortable rhythm. Review the corresponding lesson in this Leader's Guide as well.

Each lesson includes the following:

- an introduction and list of learning objectives that expand on the theme being addressed
- guidelines for reading and teaching the poems in the children's book, along with discussion questions
- one or two activities to do with the children
- suggestions for follow-up activities to sustain and reinforce the ideas in the lesson
- additional children's literature and, in some cases, other resources for adults related to the lesson theme.

Some of the lessons also include reproducible Home Handouts to send home to parents or caregivers.

We think you'll find the poems and activities both effective and fun. In addition to building self-esteem and responsibility in children, the lessons can provide many benefits for *you.* They will allow you an opportunity to get to know your students better. As you encourage children to care about each other, cooperate, and resolve conflicts themselves, your classroom can become more peaceful and productive. You'll have the satisfaction of helping children develop and practice skills they'll use for a lifetime.

We've had a wonderful time working with our students and colleagues to develop the activities in this Leader's Guide. We hope you enjoy sharing them with children as much as we've enjoyed creating them.

Judy Lalli
Mary Martha Whitworth

Dear Parent/Caregiver,

Our group is about to begin an exciting new program designed to help children learn to value themselves and appreciate and get along with other people.

The program is based on a book called *I Like Being Me: Poems for Children About Feeling Special, Appreciating Others, and Getting Along*. This book uses short, easy-to-read poems and appealing photographs to help children think about and understand ideas like believing in themselves, learning from mistakes, being dependable, cooperating, and being a friend. The lessons include questions and activities that reinforce these ideas in ways that are fun for everyone.

From time to time, your child will bring home handouts related to the lessons. These handouts will tell you more about the ideas we'll be exploring so you can talk about them with your child.

We'll begin the program on ____________________(date). If you have any questions, please feel free to call me.

Sincerely,

____

Telephone: ______________________

LESSON 1

Having a Positive Attitude

People can look at the same situation in different ways. We need to make children aware that they can become more positive in their thinking, especially about themselves. We can help them choose a more positive outlook.

Goals

1. To teach children that they can choose to look on the brighter side of many situations.
2. To help children discover that being positive helps them feel good about themselves.
3. To encourage children to develop a positive attitude.

Reading and Discussing the Poem

I Can Choose

I can choose
To win or lose.
I know it's up to me.

If I think that
I'm a winner,
That's what I will be!

Materials needed:

- Clear glass filled halfway with water

Before reading the poem, show the children the glass filled halfway with water. Say to the children, "Look at this glass. Some people might say it's half empty, and some others might say it's half full. Raise your hand if you think this glass is half empty. Raise your hand if you think the glass is half full."

Invite the children to explain their answers. Be sure to discuss both points of view. Then say, "Some people said the glass was half empty, and some said it was half full. Both answers are true. Sometimes people look at things in different ways. Now let's listen to a poem about looking at things in different ways."

Read the poem to the children and show the accompanying photograph. Ask questions like:

- "Do you think the child in the picture thinks of himself as a winner or a loser? How can you tell?"
- "Why do you think the poem says 'If I think that I'm a winner, that's what I will be'?"
- "Can you think of a time when you thought of yourself as a winner? Tell us about it."

If you wish, explain the lesson theme: having a positive attitude. You might say, "People who think of themselves as winners often have a *positive attitude*. What does it mean to have a positive attitude?"

At the end of this discussion, invite the children to recite the poem with you.

Activity: The Brighter Side

Materials needed:

- Index cards on which you've written one scenario per card (see below)
- *Optional:* White 8½″ × 11″ paper; crayons, colored pencils, and/or markers

Write each of the following scenarios on an index card (or create and write scenarios appropriate for the children in your group):

- It rains on the day of the class picnic.

- You lose your ice cream money.
- A good friend moves away.
- The TV isn't working.
- You didn't get a part in the class play.
- Your favorite snack isn't in the cupboard.
- Your cousin comes to visit and doesn't want to play the game you planned.

Explain the activity. One child chooses a card and reads, or asks someone else to read, the sentence. Each sentence describes something that at first might seem bad. Then the group thinks of as many "brighter sides" as possible. For example, if a card says "You break your arm skateboarding," some "brighter sides" might be:

- The other kids can decorate my cast.
- I won't have to do chores for a while.
- I'll get some extra attention.

At the end of the activity, ask the children, "How can looking on the brighter side help you be a winner?" Include in your discussion the point that finding "brighter sides" helps people have a positive attitude.

Optional: Invite the children to draw pictures showing "brighter sides" of different situations and, if they wish, to write or dictate sentences explaining their pictures.

Follow-up

1. Incorporate positive expressions into your group's vocabulary. Talk about looking at the glass as half full, at the brighter side of things, at the "silver lining" in the clouds. When negative things happen, help the children find a positive aspect. Have a positive attitude yourself, too! Use positive phrasing when talking to students. Tell them what you *do* want them to do ("Please walk") instead of what you *don't* want them to do ("Don't run"). Your optimism will create a positive mood that's "catching."
2. Bring smiles to the children's faces every morning with a "Joke of the Day." Set aside a time for telling a joke or riddle. A terrific source is *Riddles in a Jar* by Deborah Stein (see "Additional Resources" below). Add to the fun by wearing a funny hat or a plastic clown nose. Soon the children will be bringing in jokes to share and asking to wear the hat or nose. This is a great way to enjoy a laugh together and start the day with a positive attitude.
3. Copy the Home Handout for this lesson, "30 Ways to Help Your Child Feel Special," to send home to parents or caregivers.

Additional Resources

Kipfer, Barbara Ann. *1,400 Things for Kids to Be Happy About* (Workman Publishing, 1994). A "workbook of happiness" that encourages children to write down and celebrate all that they have to be happy about.

Stein, Deborah. *Riddles in a Jar* (Honor Press, 1992). A year's supply of giggle-provoking riddles that children (and adults) will love. Inquire or order by fax: (612) 397-8119.

Zemach, Margot. *It Could Always Be Worse* (Farrar, Straus & Giroux: A Sunburst Book, 1990). This Yiddish folktale teaches that it's easier to look at things in a positive light if we realize that they could always be worse.

For adults: Seligman, Martin. *The Optimistic Child* (Houghton Mifflin, 1995). Provides teachers and parents with strategies for building optimism, self-confidence, and resiliency in children.

30 Ways to Help Your Child Feel Special

Every child is special, and every child deserves to know this. Feeling special helps children believe in themselves and have a positive outlook. Here are 30 simple things you can do at home to help your child feel special:

1. Start each day with a smile.
2. Tell your child why she/he is special to you.
3. Say "I love you" often.
4. Share jokes or funny stories and laugh together.
5. Help your child see the brighter side of difficult situations.
6. Say "I'm glad you're part of this family."
7. Really listen to your child.
8. Attend your child's school events, performances, and sports activities.
9. Ask "What do you think?"
10. Treat your child with respect, as you'd treat a good friend.
11. Be aware that name-calling, teasing, and embarrassing remarks can be hurtful to your child.
12. Say "You can do it."
13. Set aside special time for your child.
14. Take walks together.
15. Say "I love spending time with you."
16. Ask your child for help.
17. Help your child learn new skills.
18. Fix meals together.
19. Do chores together. Say "Thanks for helping."
20. Whenever possible, say "Please do this" instead of "Don't do that."
21. Read books together.
22. Do fun things together.
23. Be silly together.
24. Notice when your child tries something new.
25. Believe in your child.
26. Say "I like you."
27. Say "I'm glad you're you."
28. Hug each other often.
29. At bedtime, talk about the good things that happened during the day.
30. Say "Sweet dreams."

LESSON 2

Being Patient

Children often have difficulty waiting for a birthday to arrive, for a teacher's attention, or for a turn in a game. We need to help children accept the fact that it's often necessary to wait. We need to help them learn to be patient.

Goals

1. To help children recognize that waiting is often necessary.
2. To help children see that getting cranky or angry won't make time go any faster.
3. To introduce ways to make waiting easier.

Reading and Discussing the Poem

I'm Waiting for a Rainbow

I'm waiting for a rainbow,
I'm waiting for the sun.
I'm waiting for the rain to stop
So I can play and run.

I know I should be patient,
But waiting's such a pain.
I guess I'll have to pass the time
Appreciating rain.

If possible, wait for a rainy day to introduce this lesson. Read the poem to the children and show the accompanying photograph. Ask questions like:

- "How do you think the children in the picture feel about the rain? Why?"
- "What are the children waiting for?"
- "What does it mean to *appreciate* something? What do you appreciate about rain?"
- "When do you have trouble waiting? What do you do to make waiting easier?"

If you wish, explain the lesson theme: being patient. You might say, "The children in the poem found a way to be *patient.* What does it mean to be patient?"

At the end of this discussion, invite the children to recite the poem with you.

Activities: 1. Waiting Chains

Materials needed:

- Construction paper
- Safety scissors
- Crayons, colored pencils, and/or markers
- Glue sticks

NOTE: This activity takes place over two days.

Day 1: Plan something exciting for the end of Day 2. Sometime during Day 1, give each child a sheet of construction paper. Explain that the children are to cut out, decorate, and glue together eight strips of paper to make a chain. Demonstrate how to cut and glue the strips into links.

Hang the chains on individual desks or cubbies or in a common area. Tell the children that you've planned something special for the next day. Explain that tomorrow they can use their chains as "waiting chains" to help them be patient while they wait for their special activity.

Day 2: Depending on your time frame, have the children remove one link per hour or half-hour.

Each time, they can count how many links they've removed and how many are left. Suggest that the children either take the used links home or put them in the recycling bin. Talk with students about how the waiting chains help them to be patient.

NOTE: You can also use this activity ten days before an important event such as a field trip, school play, or holiday. Have the children make ten links and remove one each day.

2. Plants Take Patience

Materials needed:

- Empty milk cartons, each with the top cut off and holes punched in the bottom
- Potting soil
- Flower seeds
- One or more trays

Planting and waiting for seeds to grow is an excellent way for children to experience being patient. Have the children fill the cartons 1/4 full of soil, and then plant flower seeds 1/2 inch below the surface. Place the cartons on a tray in a warm, sunny place and have the children water them according to the directions on the seed package.

Remind the children to be patient as they eagerly await the first signs of growth. Observe and discuss the changes that occur as the seeds begin to sprout. Talk about the pleasure that comes with waiting for the seeds to sprout and grow. Point out to the children that they are learning to be patient.

Once the seeds have sprouted, you may want to let the children take their plants home.

Follow-up

1. Clearly communicate time frames to the children. Use visual aids, such as calendars and time lines, to let them know how long it will be until a specific event: "Look at the calendar. Today is Tuesday. We have two more days before the open house." "It's 11:00. You'll have lunch in 20 minutes."
2. On a rainy day when the children are unable to play outside, ask them to contribute to a list of things that would be fun and appropriate to do inside instead. Emphasize that there are ways we can appreciate what we have here and now while we're waiting for something else—this helps us to be patient. Encourage the children to brainstorm as many ideas as possible. Then guide the group in choosing activities to enjoy indoors. Post the list for use on future rainy days.

Additional Resources

Kraus, Robert. *Leo the Late Bloomer* (HarperCollins, 1971). A mother lion encourages her husband to be patient while waiting for their cub to develop new skills like the other young lions.

Kraus, Ruth. *The Carrot Seed* (Harper & Row, 1945). A little boy plants a seed and waits patiently for a carrot to emerge.

Waddell, Martin. *Owl Babies* (Candlewick Press, 1993). Three baby owls wait for their mother to return to the nest with food. The youngest owl becomes impatient, worrying that the mother will never return, and needs to be reassured by his older siblings.

LESSON 3

Listening

Children do many kinds of listening. They listen to music, to directions, and to their friends. Children need to understand that there is more to listening than merely hearing sounds. We can help them develop, practice, and improve their listening skills.

Goals

1. To teach children ways to show interest and attention while listening.
2. To help children understand how listening helps them learn.
3. To guide children to become better listeners.

Reading and Discussing the Poem

I Hear the Music Playing

I hear the music playing,
But I don't remember the song.

I hear the teacher talking,
But I get the directions wrong.

I hear the children reading,
But I miss where to follow along.

My hearing seems to be okay,
But my listening isn't strong.

Read the poem to the children and show the accompanying photograph. Read it a few more times, encouraging the children to recite it along with you as they learn it.

Next, explain the idea of responsive reading, in which readers read alternate lines of a poem. Help the children read the poem responsively with you: Recite the first line yourself; have the children recite the second line; recite the third line; have the children recite the fourth; and so on.

Ask questions like:

- "Why do you think the person in the poem doesn't remember the song?"
- "Why do you think the person gets the directions wrong?"
- "How can someone hear without really listening?"
- "Can you think of a time when it would be important to listen very carefully? Tell us about it."
- "How do you know when someone is really listening to you? How do you feel when someone does this?"

If you wish, explain the lesson theme: listening. You might say, "This poem is about *listening*. There's more to listening than just hearing someone's words. What does it mean to really listen?"

Activities: 1. Listening Walk

Materials needed:

- Chart paper and easel (or tape the paper to a chalkboard or wall)
- Marker
- *Optional: The Listening Walk* by Paul Showers (see "Additional Resources," page 11)

If you have *The Listening Walk*, read the story to the group to set the stage for this activity.

Take the children outside for a "listening walk." Explain that everyone will walk in silence for five minutes and listen for all the sounds they can hear. Briefly describe the different types of sounds the children might hear: nature sounds (such as birds chirping, leaves rustling, or wind blowing), traffic sounds (such as horns honking or tires screeching), people sounds (such as children shouting as they play or babies crying), and so forth.

After five minutes, stop and ask the children what sounds they've heard. Then say, "Let's walk for five minutes more. This time, listen for any *new* sounds."

Walk for another five minutes. Stop again and ask the children what new sounds they've heard. If you wish, repeat the process one more time, again having the children listen for different sounds.

Return indoors. Together, make a list of all the sounds the children heard on their walk. Talk about the new things they heard as they listened more and more carefully.

2. Whisper Down the Lane

This is a familiar childhood game that demonstrates how messages often get changed as they pass from one person to another.

Divide the group into teams of six to eight players. Have each team stand in a circle or row to form a "lane." Explain that you will whisper the same phrase to the first person on each team. Tell the children that you'll whisper it to each person *only once*, and that person is to whisper it *only once* to the next person on the team, with no repeating allowed. Team members will continue to whisper the phrase "down the lane" from one player to the next. The last person on the team (the one at the "end of the lane") should then act out the phrase. This isn't a contest; the goal is to have fun while improving listening skills.

Suggested phrases to "whisper":

- "Tap your head four times."
- "Hold your elbows with your opposite hands."
- "Spin around two times, then touch the ground."

It's fun to observe the different actions that each person performs. Emphasize that no single person is responsible for the final result. Practice with this game will lead to better listening. Challenge *all* teams to get the directions right by listening carefully.

Follow-up

1. Show the children a "listening position" in which they sit quietly and look at the speaker. Teach them to ask the speaker questions if there's something they don't understand. Remember to model this yourself!
2. During discussions, occasionally ask questions like, "Who can tell us what Tomás just said?"
3. When reading a story to the group, encourage the children to provide appropriate sound effects, such as wind blowing, leaves crunching, dogs barking, or babies crying. Develop a signal between you and the children so they'll know when it's appropriate for them to provide the sounds. To encourage even more precise listening, divide students into groups and assign different sound effects: some children bark when the dog is mentioned, others are the crying babies, and so forth.

Additional Resources

Aardema, Verna. *Bringing the Rain to Kapiti Plain* (Dial Press, 1983). This African tale uses repetitive, ever-longer rhymes that children enjoy listening for and reciting.

Lester, Helen. *Listen, Buddy* (Houghton Mifflin, 1995). A lop-eared rabbit finds himself in funny situations—and eventually in trouble—because he doesn't listen carefully.

Showers, Paul. *The Listening Walk* (HarperCollins, 1991). A little girl and her father take a quiet walk together and identify the sounds around them in the neighborhood and in the park.

For adults: Faber, Adele, and Elaine Mazlish. *How to Talk So Kids Will Listen and Listen So Kids Will Talk* (Avon Books, 1982). This easy-to-read, comprehensive guide is accompanied by cartoons and realistic vignettes. An invaluable resource for anyone who lives or works with children.

LESSON 4

Believing in Myself

Everyone lacks confidence occasionally. When we're able to keep trying and then accomplish a task, we tend to gain confidence. We need to show children that we believe in them and in their abilities. This helps them feel more sure of themselves and be more willing to try things.

Goals

1. To make children aware that everyone is afraid to try sometimes.
2. To help children understand that if they don't try, they can't succeed.
3. To encourage children to believe in themselves and be more willing to try things.

Reading and Discussing the Poem

I Didn't Believe I Could Do It

I didn't believe I could do it.
I was afraid to try.
My *teacher* believed I could do it,
And next time, so will I.

Show the children the photograph. Ask questions like:

- "How do you think the girl feels about the pattern she created with the blocks?"
- "Do you think at first she believed she'd be able to make it?"

Read the poem to the children. Read it again and ask them to recite it along with you. They will probably be able to memorize it easily. Ask questions like:

- "Why do you think the girl in the poem didn't believe she could do it?"
- "Why did the teacher believe the girl could do it?"
- "Did anyone ever keep telling you that you could do something, even though you thought you couldn't? Did the person help change the way you felt? How?"
- "Did you ever think you couldn't do something and then find out you could do it? How did you feel?"

If you wish, explain the lesson theme: believing in myself. You might say, "At first, the girl in the poem didn't *believe in herself*. Who helped her believe in herself? Why is it important to believe in yourself?"

Activity: Me Trees

Materials needed:

- Copies of the "Me Tree" handout on page 14
- Crayons, colored pencils, and/or markers

Give each child a copy of the "Me Tree" handout and say something like, "All of you can do many things. A 'Me Tree' is a way to show people what you can do. Write your name on the tree trunk. On each branch, write or draw a picture of something you can do."

When the children have finished, have them share their trees with the group. Display the trees in a special place.

Follow-up

1. Keep the "Me Trees" available. At various times throughout the year, say to the children: "Look at your trees. You've learned to do many things. Draw one more branch onto your tree and add one more thing that you can do."
2. From time to time, take a few minutes to play the "I Can" game. You might say: "Think of something you can do. When I call on you, say, 'I can _________,' and say something you can do. For example, you might say, 'I can ride a bike.'" Call on everyone who volunteers. Play the game often with the children. In between times, remind them that they can be thinking of things they *can do* for the next time you play the game.
3. Help the children gain confidence in their abilities by constantly telling them that you believe in them. Use phrases like:
   - "Keep at it."
   - "I know it's hard."
   - "You can do it."
   - "Remember last time when you thought you couldn't do it? And you did it!"
   - "I believe in you."

   When children succeed at something, say, "You must feel very proud."

Additional Resources

Hoffman, Mary. *Amazing Grace* (Dial Books for Young Readers, 1991). With her grandmother's support and her own faith in herself, Grace overcomes barriers of race and gender discrimination to win a part in the school play.

Martin, Bill Jr., and John Archambault. *Knots on a Counting Rope* (Henry Holt & Co., 1987). Challenged by blindness, a young Native American boy receives strength and encouragement from his grandfather, who tells him how special he is.

Polacco, Patricia. *Thunder Cake* (Philomel Books, 1990). A young girl overcomes her fear of thunderstorms as she bravely gathers ingredients to help her grandmother make a "thunder cake."

For adults: Canfield, Jack, and Harold Clive Wells. *100 Ways to Enhance Self-Concept in the Classroom: A Handbook for Teachers, Counselors, and Group Leaders*, 2d ed. (Allyn & Bacon, 1994). This all-inclusive resource contains activities, cartoons, quotations, illustrations, and stories designed to help children feel better about themselves.

LESSON 4 HANDOUT

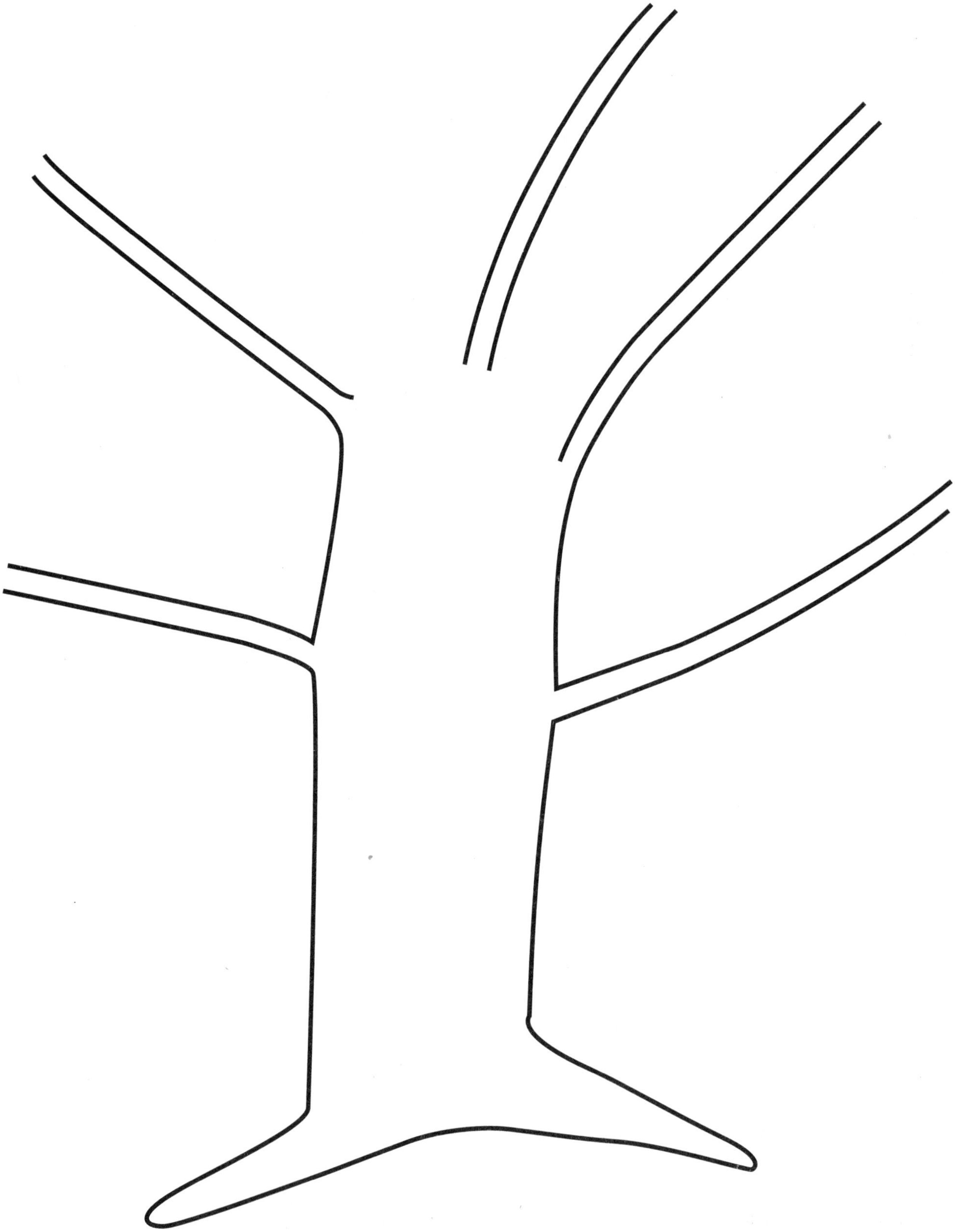

LESSON 5

Learning from Mistakes

We all make mistakes. Many children are afraid to make mistakes because they fear being judged or reprimanded. Children need to know that it's okay to make mistakes. With our help, they can begin to accept their mistakes and learn from them.

Goals

1. To help children recognize that everyone makes mistakes.
2. To emphasize that it's okay to make mistakes.
3. To demonstrate how children can learn from their mistakes.

Reading and Discussing the Poem

Mistakes Can Be Good

Mistakes can be good.
They can help you grow.
They can show you what you need
to know.

So whenever you make a mistake,
Just say:
"Now I'll try another way."

Read the poem to the children and show the accompanying photograph. Read it a few more times, encouraging the children to recite it along with you. Ask questions like:

- "What is the child in the picture doing? Do you think she ever makes a mistake? What do you think happens then?"
- "How do you usually feel when you make a mistake? Why do you feel that way?"
- "Do you agree with the poem that mistakes can be good? Why or why not?"
- "Did you ever make a mistake and then learn something from it? Can you tell us about it?"

If you wish, explain the lesson theme: learning from mistakes. You might say, "Everybody makes mistakes. The poem is about making mistakes and *learning* from them."

Activities: 1. Mistake Role Plays

Materials needed:

- Index cards on which you've written one scenario per card (see below)

Write each of the following scenarios on an index card (or create and write scenarios appropriate for the children in your group):

- You pull too hard on your jacket zipper and it gets stuck.
- You pour a cup of juice too fast and it spills.
- You forget and leave your tuna sandwich on the counter, and your cat jumps up and eats it.
- You drop your permission slip in a puddle and it gets soaked.
- You rub too hard with your eraser and the page tears.
- You don't wash your hands after you paint, and you get paint on your shirt.
- You leave the calculator on and the battery runs down.

Explain the activity. One child chooses a card and reads the sentence, or asks someone else to read it. Each sentence describes a mistake somebody could easily make. The child acts out the scene described on the card. (If more than one person is needed for a role play, call on another child to take part.)

After each role play, ask questions like:

- "What was the mistake?"
- "What might Emma have learned from this mistake?"
- "What might she do differently next time?"

2. "Mistake" Pictures

Materials needed:

- Drawing paper
- Paints and paintbrushes

Explain that the children will paint pictures that start with a "mistake." Distribute paper, paint, and paintbrushes. Say something like, "To start your picture, you're going to make a 'mistake'—on purpose! Dip your brush into the paint and dribble some paint onto your paper. Dribble it so it looks like you've spilled a glob of paint. Don't do anything else yet—just make your dribble."

Next, ask the children to create pictures from the "mistakes." Suggest that the children create their own pictures or that they trade papers and create pictures from someone else's "mistake."

Talk about the drawings. Discuss the fact that people can accomplish things they're pleased with even after making mistakes along the way.

Follow-up

1. Show acceptance, with both your statements and your nonverbal reactions, when children struggle or make mistakes. Help them explore various strategies for correcting their mistakes.
2. Admit to the children when you've made a mistake. Talk with them about what you might be able to learn from it. For example, "I didn't ask you to line up on time, and we were late for music class. Next time, I'll ask you to get ready earlier."
3. Copy the Home Handout for this lesson, "Everybody Makes Mistakes," to send home to parents or caregivers.

Additional Resources

DeCesare, Angela. *Anthony, the Perfect Monster* (Random House, 1996). When Anthony discovers that he can't be perfect in everything, he becomes a monster—until his teacher convinces him that he's okay just the way he is.

Jones, Charlotte Foltz. *Mistakes That Worked* (Doubleday, 1991). This is a collection of true stories about mistakes that turned into great inventions, including chocolate chip cookies, Frisbees, ice cream cones, and pizza.

Lindbergh, Reeve. *If I'd Known Then What I Know Now* (Puffin Books, 1996). A "do-it-yourself" dad learns from the mistakes he makes while building and fixing things.

Viorst, Judith. *My Mama Says There Aren't Any Zombies, Ghosts, Vampires, Creatures, Demons, Monsters, Fiends, Goblins, or Things* (Aladdin Paperbacks, 1988). A young boy discovers that adults—even his own mother—can make mistakes.

Everybody Makes Mistakes

We all make mistakes. Sometimes children are afraid to admit when they make a mistake. They're afraid they'll get in trouble. But mistakes are an important way people learn. Children need to know that mistakes are okay. Here are three ways you can help your child accept mistakes and learn from them:

1. When your child makes a mistake, try not to criticize or show anger. Instead, talk about the mistake:

   "Oops! You spilled a bottle of soda."

   If possible, help your child fix it:

   "Let's get some towels and soapy water so we can clean this up."

   Talk together about what your child can learn from the mistake:

   "What can you do next time to help you not spill?"

2. When *you* make a mistake, tell your child about it. Talk about what you've learned from it:

   "I couldn't find my keys, and I was late for work.
   So I'm putting a hook here on the wall.
   I can get in the habit of hanging my keys here.
   Then I won't need to look all over for them."

   Remind your child often that everybody makes mistakes.

3. Have fun learning about other people's mistakes. Do this when you and your child are with friends or other family members. Ask people to tell about funny mistakes they've made and what they've learned from their mistakes. This is a great opportunity for your child to learn that all people—even grownups—make mistakes!

LESSON 6

Persevering

It takes practice to master new skills. Some children become frustrated as they struggle to learn. We can help children realize that perseverance is a necessary part of the learning process. We can help them be more willing to keep trying and practicing.

Goals

1. To make children aware that learning takes time and practice.
2. To help children understand that persevering is important, even when they feel like giving up.
3. To demonstrate that children will feel successful as they improve a little at a time.
4. To encourage children to become more willing to persevere as they practice and learn new skills.

Reading and Discussing the Poem

At Least I'm Getting Better

I run and run and run and run,
And then I trip and fall.
I throw and catch and throw and catch,
And then I drop the ball.

I write my name and write my name,
And then I miss a letter.
But everybody makes mistakes.
At least I'm getting better!

Read the title of the poem. Say, "This is a poem about practicing and learning to do things, even when you make mistakes along the way. I'm going to read a line and then ask you to *predict* what happens next."

Read the first line. Ask, "What do you think happens after the person in the poem has been running and running?" After hearing some of the children's guesses, read the line as written. Continue, inviting the children to predict what happens to the person after throwing and catching a lot, and after writing a lot.

When you get to the last line of the poem, read it once and then have the children repeat it with you. Together, recite the entire poem again and show the photograph. Ask questions like:

- "Can you tell about a time when you kept practicing and working at something? What happened? Did you make mistakes along the way? If so, what did you do then?"
- "How did you feel when you kept practicing?"
- "Did you get better and better at what you were doing? If so, how did you feel as you got better at it?"

Children love to act out this poem. Ask students to stand and perform the motions as they recite the poem with you:

I run and run and run and run,
(run silently in place)
And then I trip and fall.
(pretend to gently "fall" in your own space)
I throw and catch and throw and catch,
(pantomime throwing and catching a ball)
And then I drop the ball.
(pantomime dropping the ball)

I write my name and write my name,
(pantomime a writing motion)
And then I miss a letter.
(pretend to be erasing a mistake)

But everybody makes mistakes.
(shrug your shoulders and hold your hands upward in an "Oh well" motion)
At least I'm getting better!
(make a "thumbs up" sign with both hands)

If you wish, explain the lesson theme: persevering. You might say, "Many things take time and practice. We need to keep trying. We need to practice over and over. Sometimes we make mistakes. When we keep trying and practicing, we're *persevering*. The poem is about *persevering* to make our skills better and better."

Activity: The Tortoise and the Hare

Materials needed:

- *Optional: The Children's Aesop* by Stephanie Calmenson (see "Additional Resources")

Many children are familiar with the fable from Aesop, "The Tortoise and the Hare," and its moral, "Slow and steady wins the race." Tell the children the name of the fable. Explain that a *hare* is a like a rabbit, but with longer ears and legs, and a *tortoise* is a turtle that lives on land. Read the fable aloud or share this version of the story:

> A hare made fun of a tortoise for being such a slow creature, so the tortoise challenged the hare to a race. Soon after the race began, the hare—who felt sure of winning—stopped to take a nap under a shady tree. Meanwhile, the tortoise kept walking along at a slow and steady pace. After a long time, the hare woke up and remembered the race. That hare ran like lightning to get to the finish line—and arrived just in time to see the tortoise cross the line and win the race!

Ask questions like:

- "The tortoise knew the hare was a faster runner. Why do you think the tortoise wanted to race the hare?"
- "Why do you think the hare felt sure of winning?"
- "Why did the hare stop to take a nap?"
- "Why was the tortoise able to win the race?"
- "What is the lesson or *moral* of the story?"

Follow-up

Give the children the gift of time. Mastering a skill takes practice—and practice takes time! Be aware, too, that children learn at different rates. Sometimes breaking tasks into smaller steps motivates children to persevere. Have a group discussion of ways to break down different tasks such as tying shoes; reading words, sentences, books, or chapters; building block structures; solving puzzles; memorizing spelling words; solving arithmetic problems; and completing projects.

Additional Resources

Calmenson, Stephanie. *The Children's Aesop: Selected Fables Retold by Stephanie Calmenson* (Boyds Mills Press, 1992). This collection of classic fables by Aesop, with its simple retelling and colorful illustrations, is geared to children.

Carlson, Nancy. *Loudmouth George and the Big Race* (Carolrhoda Books, 1983). In this modern-day version of "The Tortoise and the Hare," George brags, puts off practicing, and makes excuses instead of training for the big race.

Piper, Watty. *The Little Engine That Could* (Platt & Munk, 1976). Little Blue Engine keeps saying "I think I can, I think I can" as she perseveres and pulls a trainload of toys over the mountain.

Seuss, Dr. (Theodor Seuss Geisel). *Oh, the Places You'll Go!* (Random Books for Young Readers, 1993). A poem in classic Dr. Seuss style, this book encourages readers to persevere throughout life as they face inevitable ups and downs along the way.

LESSON 7

Liking Myself

One of the most important things we can do as teachers and parents is to help children develop self-esteem. Children are empowered when they can like themselves—not because of the way they look or what they achieve, but because they are unique, special individuals. We can help children feel comfortable saying "I like myself because I'm me."

Goals

1. To help children feel special.
2. To help children acknowledge their own uniqueness.
3. To help children value themselves as human beings.

Reading and Discussing the Poem

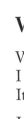

Who Should I Be?

Who should I be on dress-up day?
I can wear a mask—
It's fun to play.

I can't decide who I should be,
Because most of the time
I like being me!

Read the poem to the children and show the accompanying photograph. Read the poem again and ask the children to recite it along with you. They will probably be able to memorize it easily. Ask questions like:

- "Do you like to wear a mask or costume or pretend you're someone else? If you do, who do you like to pretend to be? Why?"
- "Why do you think the child in the poem is having trouble deciding who he should be?"
- "The child in the poem says, 'Most of the time I like being me.' What do *you* like most about being *you*?"

If you wish, explain the lesson theme: liking myself. You might say, "Each of us is special. Each of us is *unique*—there's no one quite like us. Sometimes it's fun to pretend to be someone else. But most of the time it's nice to *like* being who we are."

Activities: 1. Mirror, Mirror

Materials needed:

- Shoe box with lid
- Mirror with dimensions smaller than the bottom surface of the shoe box
- Glue stick

Glue the mirror to the inside bottom of the shoe box and close the lid.

Have the children sit in a circle. Explain that they will pass the box around. As it is passed from person to person, each child is to open the box, look inside, and say:

"Mirror, mirror, I can't wait—
Show me someone really great!"

Then the child is to tell the group about a special quality of the person in the mirror.

At the end of the activity, talk about the many different special qualities the children identified.

NOTE: As with any sharing activity of this kind, be sure to include a "pass" option.

2. Group "I Like Me" Book

Materials needed:

- White 8½″ × 11″ paper
- Crayons, colored pencils, and/or markers
- Two sheets of heavy 8½″ × 11″ paper or cardboard (for the book's cover)
- Paper punch
- Yarn or metal rings (for binding the book)
- *Optional: I Like Me!* by Nancy Carlson (see "Additional Resources"); laminating equipment

This activity reinforces children's self-respect and builds mutual respect as well. If you have *I Like Me!*, read the story to the group to set the stage for the activity.

Give each child paper and crayons, colored pencils, or markers. Tell the children to write their names on the paper. Then say something like, "Draw a picture that shows something you like about yourself. Then think of a sentence that tells about why you like being you."

Have the children write their sentences or dictate them to you or to another child.

If you want, create your own page, too. Also create a cover for the book that includes the title ("I Like Me!") and the authors (your group). When students have finished drawing and writing, compile the drawings and sentences into a book. If possible, laminate the pages before you fasten them together.

Make the book available in the library area, where it will be one of the most popular books!

Follow-up

1. Take advantage of "teachable moments" when children discover their own unique, special qualities. For example, if a child really enjoyed a math game, say to the child, "Wow! You really liked playing numbers lotto, didn't you?" When a child shares a story from home, say something like this to the group: "Suni was a big help to her family. She likes helping people. That's a way that Suni likes being Suni!"
2. Use a permanent marker to write sentence starters related to the lesson theme on each section of a beach ball. (Examples: "Something that makes me happy is __________." "My favorite place is __________.") Have the children sit in a circle and toss the ball. When a child catches the ball, have the child complete the sentence beneath his or her right thumb. Summarize what each child says: "Leo feels really good when he sits and reads with his grandpa." "Sasha's favorite place is her climbing tree at the park."

Additional Resources

Carlson, Nancy. *I Like Me!* (Penguin Books, 1988). A little pig takes good care of herself, takes responsibility for her feelings and actions, and likes herself just the way she is.

Loomans, Diane. *The Lovables in the Kingdom of Self-Esteem* (H.J. Kramer, 1991). Through rhyme and beautiful illustrations, the "Lovables"—24 animals—teach children the many ways in which they are special.

Payne, Lauren Murphy, and Claudia Rohling. *Just Because I Am: A Child's Book of Affirmation* and *A Leader's Guide to Just Because I Am* (Free Spirit Publishing Inc., 1994). The simple text and appealing illustrations of the children's book strengthen and support a child's self-esteem. The companion Leader's Guide contains lessons, follow-up questions, reading lists, and reproducibles for teachers and parents.

LESSON 8

Solving Problems

When faced with problems, some children give up or deal with them in inappropriate ways. We want to make children aware that they are capable of finding solutions to many of their problems.

Goals

1. To make children aware that they can take action toward solving many of their problems.
2. To help children recognize that there is often more than one way to solve a problem.
3. To encourage children to take pride in solving problems themselves.
4. To help children become more willing to deal with and solve problems.

Reading and Discussing the Poem

Broken Wagon

I'm mad.
It looks bad.
I think I broke my wagon.

It has a dent.
The wheel is bent.
And everything is draggin'.

The handle's loose.
Oh, what's the use?
I hope somebody kicks it.

I want to shout
And throw it out!
But I think I'd better fix it.

Before reading the poem, show the children the photograph and say, "This boy broke his wagon. What are some ways he could deal with this problem?" Seek a variety of responses.

Read the poem to the children. Ask questions like:

- "What are some things the boy wants to do about the broken wagon?"
- "Which ways would solve the problem? Which ways wouldn't? Why?"
- "How do you think the boy could fix his wagon?"
- "Think of a problem you've had. What did you do about it? Did you solve your problem?"

If you wish, explain the lesson theme: solving problems. You might say, "The boy in the poem has a problem. He's trying to decide how to *solve his problem*. Often there's more than one way to solve a problem. When you have a problem, you can think about some good ways of solving it."

Activity: A Class Problem

Materials needed:

- Chart paper and easel (or tape the paper to a chalkboard or wall)
- Marker

Talk with the children about a problem that the group is having. (If you're lucky enough not to have a problem, make one up!) Tell the group that you can all work together to solve the problem. Start by brainstorming a list of possible solutions. Say something like, "I think we can solve this problem together. First, we need to think of lots of different ideas for solving the problem. To do this, we can use a special skill called *brainstorming*. When we *brainstorm*, we try to think of all the ideas we can. As you think of ideas, I'll write them on a chart.

"The rule in brainstorming is that *all* ideas are written down. We don't say 'Great idea!' We don't say 'That won't work!' We don't say *anything* about whether we think an idea will work. Deciding what will work comes later. We just think up ideas and write them down."

As the children suggest solutions, list them on the chart paper. Remind students that no one is to criticize or praise anyone else's ideas while the list is being made. Because all ideas must be listed without comment, children feel free to stretch their minds in coming up with new and different responses.

After the list is completed, lead the group in a discussion of the various solutions and which ones might work best. Encourage the children to really *listen* to each other's ideas and to remain respectful.

Follow-up

1. Provide plenty of opportunities for children to come up with their own solutions to problems. For example, if a child says, "My pencil is broken," ask, "What are you going to do?" Encourage the child to think of short-term solutions (such as sharpening the pencil or borrowing one from a friend) and long-term solutions (such as bringing more pencils from home).
2. Allow children the time they need to deal with their problems, rather than rushing in to help. It's okay for children to experience a reasonable amount of struggling, whether it involves pulling up a zipper, looking for a lost item, or thinking of an answer to a challenging question. Praise effort as much as results! Children will feel more confident the next time they're confronted with a problem if they've previously experienced the satisfaction of dealing with problems on their own.
3. While reading or telling stories to the children, point out the problems the characters face and the ways in which they solve them. Soon, you can begin to ask the children to identify the problems in the stories and to predict how the characters will solve them.

Additional Resources

Duke, Kate. *Aunt Isabel Tells a Good One* (Penguin Books, 1992). A mouse princess solves the problem of rescuing the prince by using her wits rather than violence.

Schwartz, Linda. *What Would You Do? A Kid's Guide to Tricky and Sticky Situations* (The Learning Works, 1990). Presents typical childhood dilemmas for children to discuss, followed by suggested solutions.

Williams, Vera B. *A Chair for My Mother* (William Morrow & Co., 1982). A young girl takes action to help her mother replace a favorite chair that was destroyed in a fire.

LESSON 9

Being Dependable

It's important to keep commitments. Whether their commitment is to care for a pet or to be ready on time, children often need to be reminded to do what they've said they'll do. We can teach children the importance of keeping commitments. We can help them understand that by showing responsibility and keeping their promises, they prove that they can be counted on in the future.

Goals

1. To help children recognize that keeping one's word shows respect and caring for others.
2. To help children recognize that when a person keeps a promise, others will know they can depend on the person in the future.
3. To reinforce the importance of being dependable.

Reading and Discussing the Poem

If I Promise to Do It

If I promise to do it,
I'll do it.

If I promise to go,
I'll be there.

If I promise to finish,
I'll finish.

Keeping my word
Shows I care.

Read the poem to the children and show the accompanying photograph. Read it a few more times, encouraging the children to recite it along with you. Its singsong rhythms will make it easy for them to learn. Ask questions like:

- "What do you think the boy on the phone is promising to do?"
- "Do you think he's going to do what he says? Why?"
- "How do you feel when someone promises to do something for you and *does* it?"
- "How do you feel when someone promises to do something for you and *doesn't* do it?"

If you wish, explain the lesson theme: being dependable. You might say, "The boy in the poem keeps his word. When we keep our word, we're *being dependable*. We're showing other people that they can count on us to do what we say we'll do."

Activity: Circle of Pride

This is a quick activity that gives children the opportunity to reflect on a time when they were dependable and to listen to other people's examples of being reliable as well.

Have the children sit in a circle. Explain that it's a "circle of pride." Go around the circle and invite the children to respond to this statement: "This is a time when I kept a promise." After each child responds, have the child conclude by saying, "I feel proud about this."

As the children share their memories, encourage discussion that helps everyone understand what it means to be dependable. For example, you might ask, "How do you think the person felt when Kavon kept his word? What might have happened if Kavon hadn't kept his word?"

NOTE: As with any sharing activity of this kind, be sure to include a "pass" option.

Follow-up

1. Encourage the children to keep their commitments and emphasize the benefits of their doing so. For example: "Everyone followed directions when the parent volunteers were here, just like you promised you would. That means we'll be able to have parent volunteers come back to help us again!"

2. Set up a system of logical consequences to follow when the children *don't* do what they've said they will do. A logical consequence relates directly to the behavior problem. It isn't meant to punish the children, but to help them learn what happens when they don't keep commitments. Examples:

   - "You agreed to play the game by the rules and you didn't, so we won't be able to play this game again for one week."
   - "You didn't rinse out the paintbrushes the last time we painted. Now they're all dried up, so we won't be able to paint today."

   Keep your voice matter-of-fact, not judgmental. Stick to the consequence you've set!

3. Display a "You Can Count on Us" chart and place a star or sticker on the chart whenever the entire group does something that shows dependability. An example might be when everyone brings in a library book on the assigned day. When the chart has accumulated a preset number of stars or stickers, reward everyone with a treat such as popcorn, special group time, or extra recess.

Additional Resources

Munsch, Robert, and Michael Kusugak. *A Promise Is a Promise* (Annick Press, 1988). An Inuit child learns the meaning of the words "A promise is a promise" after she encounters imaginary Arctic creatures under the ice.

Rope, Peter, and Connie Rope. *Keep the Lights Burning, Abbie* (Carolrhoda Books, 1985). A young girl who lives in a lighthouse promises her father that she'll keep the lights burning while he's away. Based on a true story.

Steig, William. *Brave Irene* (Farrar, Straus & Giroux, 1986). A girl overcomes many obstacles to keep her word to her mother.

LESSON 10

Telling the Truth

We constantly emphasize to children the importance of telling the truth. Yet we know—and they know—that sometimes this is very hard to do. We need to help children understand that there are good reasons for telling the truth.

Goals

1. To reinforce the idea that when children consistently tell the truth, other people are more likely to trust them.
2. To encourage children to choose to tell the truth.

Reading and Discussing the Poem

Grandma Says

Grandma says I shouldn't lie,
The truth is always better.
I just hope she doesn't ask
If I like my birthday sweater.

Read the poem to the children and have them recite it with you a few times. Ask:

- "Why do you think the grandma in the poem taught the boy that it's important to tell the truth?"
- "Has anyone ever taught you that it's important to tell the truth? Who?"
- "Do you think people feel better when they tell the truth? Why or why not?"

Show the photograph of the boy opening the box. Ask:

- "Do you think the boy likes the present? Why or why not?"
- "Why does the boy hope his grandma won't ask him if he likes the sweater?"
- "What do you think he's going to tell her if she asks him? Why?"
- "If you were the boy, what would you tell her? Why?"
- "Have you ever worried that telling the truth might hurt somebody's feelings? What did you do? What happened?"

Talk about the fact that telling the truth isn't always easy, but it's still important to be honest so people will trust us. The children might also want to discuss truthful things the boy can say to his grandma that won't hurt her feelings.

If you wish, explain the lesson theme: telling the truth. You might say, "The grandmother in the poem says the truth is always better. Sometimes it's hard to *tell the truth*, but the more we do, the more people will trust us."

Activity: The Boy Who Cried Wolf

Materials needed:

- *Optional: The Children's Book of Virtues* by William J. Bennett (see "Additional Resources," page 27)

Many children are familiar with the fable from Aesop called "The Boy Who Cried Wolf." The fable is included in *The Children's Book of Virtues*. Read the fable aloud or share this version of the story:

A young shepherd was tending his sheep alone in a field. He thought it would be fun to play a trick on the villagers, so he ran toward the village crying, "Wolf! Wolf! Come and help!" The villagers dropped everything and came running at once to save the boy and the sheep from the wolf. When they arrived, the boy laughed at them, for there was no wolf at all! The villagers were very angry. They warned the boy not to call for help unless he was truly in trouble.

A few days later, the boy repeated his prank. He cried, "Wolf! Wolf!" again, and once more the villagers came running to his aid. Once more he laughed at them, and they realized that he had not been telling the truth.

A few days after that, a wolf *did* appear. It began to attack the sheep. The boy cried, "Wolf! Wolf!" again and again. But this time the villagers were sure that the boy was lying about the wolf. Nobody came to his rescue, and all of the sheep were killed.

Ask questions like:

- "Why didn't the villagers believe the boy when he cried 'Wolf!' the third time?"
- "What is the lesson or *moral* of the story?"

This is a story that is easy and fun for the children to act out. Invite volunteers to play the parts of the boy, the sheep, the villagers, and the wolf. Suggest that the children either pantomime the actions as you retell the story or speak the parts of the characters themselves.

Follow-up

1. Tell the truth yourself as often as possible. For example, if you forget to bring the treats you promised, don't tell the children that there were none in the store. Admit that you forgot.
2. Provide positive reinforcement when the children tell the truth. You might say, "I appreciate your honesty. Being truthful lets people know they can trust you."

Additional Resources

Bennett, William J. *The Children's Book of Virtues* (Simon & Schuster, 1995). "The Boy Who Cried Wolf" is one of the many classic children's tales Bennett uses to teach virtues.

Bourgeois, Paulette. *Franklin Fibs* (Scholastic, 1991). A turtle named Franklin brags about doing something that he really can't do, and then has to deal with the consequences.

Rothenberg, Joan. *Yettele's Feathers* (Hyperion Paperbacks for Children, 1996). A rabbi teaches Yettele a lesson about the hurt that can be caused when someone spreads untrue stories.

Sharmat, Marjorie. *The Big Fat Enormous Lie* (Puffin Books, 1986). A young boy tells a little lie, and the lie turns into a creature that grows and grows all day.

LESSON 11

Being Kind

Words are very powerful. Name-calling and teasing can have a lasting effect on children. Children need to understand that unkind words hurt people's feelings.

Goals

1. To reinforce the idea that unkind words and name-calling can cause hurt feelings.
2. To increase children's awareness of how they are treating others.
3. To encourage children not to use hurtful words.
4. To encourage children to be kind to each other.

Reading and Discussing the Poem

Don't Say "Crybaby!"

Don't say "Crybaby!"
Don't say "Dummy!"
Teasing makes me
Feel so crummy.

Falling down
Can bruise my knees,
But words can hurt
Where no one sees.

Show the children the photograph. Ask questions like:

- "Why do you think one girl is holding her ears?"
- "How do you think she's feeling? What makes you think that?"
- "What do you think the other girl might be saying?"

Read the poem to the children. Read it again and ask them to recite it along with you. They will probably be able to memorize it easily. Ask the children for a show of hands in response to these questions:

- "How many of you have ever been teased?"
- "How many of you like to be teased?"

Continue the discussion by asking questions like:

- "Think of a time when someone teased you. How did you feel?"
- "Did you tell the person how you felt? What did you say? What happened next?"
- "Instead of teasing, what would you have liked the person to say to you?"
- "What can you do when people tease you?"

If you wish, explain the lesson theme: being kind. You might say, "Teasing can hurt people. *Being kind* helps people feel good. What does it mean to be kind? What are some ways people are kind to each other?"

Activity: A Story About How Words Can Hurt*

Materials needed:

- Copies of the "I Like Being Me" and "Faces" handouts on pages 31 and 32
- Crayons, colored pencils, and/or markers
- Safety scissors
- Tape

* "A Story About How Words Can Hurt" is adapted from the IALAC ("I Am Lovable And Capable") story written by Sidney B. Simon, and is used with his permission. For the full version of the IALAC story and information on how to obtain the filmstrip or the video, call Values Press, (413) 296-4001.

- Paper punch
- Yarn or string

Make two signs for yourself: For each, cut out the ten faces from the "Faces" handout and tape them to the "I Like Being Me" sign. If you wish, color or decorate the signs. Punch holes as indicated and attach yarn or string.

Hang one of the signs around your neck. Invite the children to tell you what the words on the sign say: "I like being me." Tell the children that you're going to read them a story about how teasing and name-calling made someone feel bad about herself.

Read the following story to the children; feel free to add or change incidents as you go along, using examples appropriate for your group. Each time you see the italicized instruction *(remove face)* in the story, take off one of the sign's smiling faces and set it nearby.

> This is the story of Marcella and her day at school. She steps off the bus wearing her "I like being me" sign. It's a nice day. Marcella walks slowly, looking around and enjoying the sunshine and warm air. Suddenly someone yells, "Hey, slowpoke, get out of my way!" and bumps against her. Marcella drops her backpack, spilling everything. She likes herself a little less. She takes one of the smiling faces off of her sign. *(remove face)*
>
> Marcella starts to pick up her things. Nobody stops to help her. *(remove face)* Someone walking by laughs and points at her and says, "Ha ha! You dropped something!" *(remove face)*
>
> During small group time, the teacher asks Marcella a question. Marcella doesn't answer, and someone whispers loud enough for everyone to hear, "She's so dumb!" *(remove face)*
>
> At lunchtime, Marcella goes to sit with a group of children. They say, "We don't want to sit with you. Go sit somewhere else." *(remove face)* Marcella starts to cry, and the kids at the table start chanting, "Crybaby, crybaby!" *(remove face)*
>
> After lunch, Marcella goes outside to play. She trips and drops her ball. Another child grabs the ball and shouts, "You dropped it—now it's mine! Girls can't play ball anyway!" *(remove face)* Marcella goes and sits by herself. She wishes someone would come and talk to her, but nobody does. *(remove face)*
>
> At the end of the day, Marcella gets on the bus to go home. She trips in the aisle and falls. Someone shouts, "What's the matter—don't you know how to walk?" Some of the kids on the bus start to laugh. *(remove face)* By the time Marcella finds a seat, only one face remains on her "I like being me" sign.

Hold up the second sign with all of the faces in place and finish the story by saying, "It's a good thing that Marcella can start the day tomorrow with a brand new sign. I hope it doesn't lose so many happy faces again—don't you?"

Give the children copies of both handouts. Suggest that they start by decorating the faces and the sign. Have them cut out the faces and tape them to their signs. Distribute yarn or string and show the children how to hang their signs around their necks. Say, "We'll each wear a sign for the rest of the day. Anytime someone says something to you that makes you feel bad, don't say anything back. Just remove one of the smiling faces from your sign. I'm going to do it, too."

Near the end of the day, say, "We're going to talk about what we learned by wearing our signs. I'm going to ask you to tell us about some of the reasons you took off faces. Please don't say *who* hurt your feelings—just tell us what happened or what words people said."

Discuss people's experiences wearing the signs. Ask questions like:

- "What kinds of things caused you to take a face off of your sign? How did you feel?"
- "Did you say anything that caused someone else to take off a face? How did you feel?"
- "What did you learn from wearing the signs?"

★Follow-up

1. Repeat the activity with a positive twist: Have the children start with a blank sign and draw a smiling face on it each time someone says something that makes them feel good.

2. Have a ground rule in your group that there will be no name-calling or put-downs. Explain that when someone teases or calls someone else a name, whoever said something hurtful should immediately say something nice to the person instead. Teach the children to let other people know when they say things that hurt their feelings.

Additional Resources

de Paola, Tomie. *Oliver Button Is a Sissy* (Harcourt Brace Jovanovich, 1979). Oliver rises above his classmates' taunts and they learn to respect his dancing ability.

Henkes, Kevin. *Chrysanthemum* (Mulberry Books, 1996). A little mouse feels sad when others tease her about her name, until she learns that a favorite teacher is named after a flower, too.

Yashima, Taro. *Crow Boy* (Puffin Books, 1976). A young Japanese boy is teased and called names by his classmates, until they discover his hidden talent.

For adults: Rice, Judith Anne. *The Kindness Curriculum: Introducing Young Children to Loving Values* (Redleaf Press, 1995). Activities help to instill character and create opportunities for children to practice kindness, empathy, conflict resolution, and respect.

LESSON 11 HANDOUT

I Like Being Me

LESSON 11 HANDOUT

LESSON 12

Dealing with Feelings

Everyone has feelings. Children need to understand that it's natural—and okay—to have all kinds of strong emotions. We need to help children find *words* to describe their feelings and *ways* to express feelings appropriately.

Goals

1. To teach children that it's okay to have feelings.
2. To help children learn words for feelings.
3. To increase children's awareness of their own and others' feelings.
4. To guide children to find appropriate ways to express feelings.

Reading and Discussing the Poem

When I'm Cranky

When I'm cranky
I sass my mother,
I stamp my feet,
I boss my brother.

I think what I should do instead
Is jog,
Or jump,
Or go to bed.

Show the children the photograph. Ask questions like:

- "What is the child in the picture doing?"
- "How do you think he's feeling?"
- "How can you tell?"

Read the poem to the children, using a forceful, "cranky" voice for the first stanza and a softer, more thoughtful voice for the second. Ask questions like:

- "Why do you think this boy might be cranky?"
- "What does he do when he feels cranky?"
- "Why does he think he should jog, or jump, or go to bed instead?"
- "When are some times you feel cranky?"
- "What do you do when you're cranky?"

Children enjoy acting out this poem. Ask students to stand and perform the motions as they recite the poem with you:

When I'm cranky
I sass my mother,
(put hands on hips and mimic sassing)
I stamp my feet,
(stamp feet)
I boss my brother.
(wag a finger in a bossy manner)

I think what I should do instead
Is jog,
(jog quickly in place)
Or jump,
(jump once)
Or go to bed.
(lie down quietly on the floor and pretend to sleep)

If you wish, explain the lesson theme: dealing with feelings. You might say, "All of us feel cranky or angry or sad sometimes. There are many ways to *deal with feelings,* and some ways are better than others. There are ways that let us get the feelings out without hurting ourselves or someone else."

Activities: 1. "Feelings" Card Game

Materials needed:

- Index cards on which you've written sentence starters (see below)

Prepare the index cards for this activity in advance. On each card, write a sentence starter that uses the format "When _______, I feel _______." Examples:

- When someone smiles at me, I feel _______.
- When no one will play with me, I feel _______.
- When I make a mistake, I feel _______.
- When I get lost, I feel _______.
- When I learn something new, I feel _______.

Prepare at least as many sentence-starter cards as there are children in your group.

One at a time, have the children draw a card. Read the card to the child or invite the child to read it aloud. Ask the child to fill in the word that tells how she or he feels.

Write a feeling word on the board and ask the children to think of some helpful ways to deal with the feeling. Suggestions for dealing with angry feelings might include the following:

- Tell somebody that you're angry.
- Cry it out.
- Run, swing, or do jumping jacks.
- Bounce a ball.

Emphasize that everyone has many strong feelings. Let the children know that both boys *and* girls can cry and feel angry.

2. "Here's How We're Feeling" Chart*

Materials needed:

- Large piece of posterboard
- Envelopes (6½″ × 3½″ or business size)
- Scissors
- Marker
- Sheets of 9″ × 12″ construction paper in yellow, blue, purple, green, orange, and red
- Stapler or glue stick

This is an excellent tool for helping children to identify their own feelings and to become more aware of other people's feelings.

Seal the envelopes and cut them in half vertically. You've just made two pockets out of each envelope. Label each pocket: one for you, one for each child, one for a visitor, and six for feelings (you may also want to draw faces to represent the six feelings, as shown in the illustration). Cut several 4½″ × 1″ strips of construction paper in each color (one sheet makes 24 strips). Attach the pockets to the posterboard. Above the feelings pockets, write the name of the chart: "Here's How We're Feeling." Place the strips in the feelings pockets as shown (yellow for "happy," blue for "sad," purple for "okay," green for "tired," orange for "worried," and red for "angry").

Hang the "Here's How We're Feeling" chart somewhere near the entrance to the room, at a level where the children can reach the pockets with their names on them. Introduce the chart by saying, "It helps to know how everyone is feeling. Here's a chart we can use to show how each of us feels right now." Have each child choose a colored strip that represents how the child is feeling and place the strip in her or his pocket. Choose a colored strip for your own pocket, too.

Follow-up

1. Replay the "Feelings" card game from time to time. Emphasize that it's okay for the children to finish the sentences differently than other people who've had the card before. Use feelings words yourself whenever appropriate. Take care to model appropriate ways to express and deal with feelings. When children express their feelings inappropriately, let them know that the feelings are acceptable but the behavior is not.

2. Keep the "Here's How We're Feeling" chart posted and use it as part of the daily routine. The chart lets you quickly assess the mood of the group as well as the feelings of individuals. It allows the children to communicate their feel-

* This activity was contributed by Jay Farrelly, elementary teacher, Stony Creek Elementary School, Blue Bell, PA. Used with permission of Jay Farrelly.

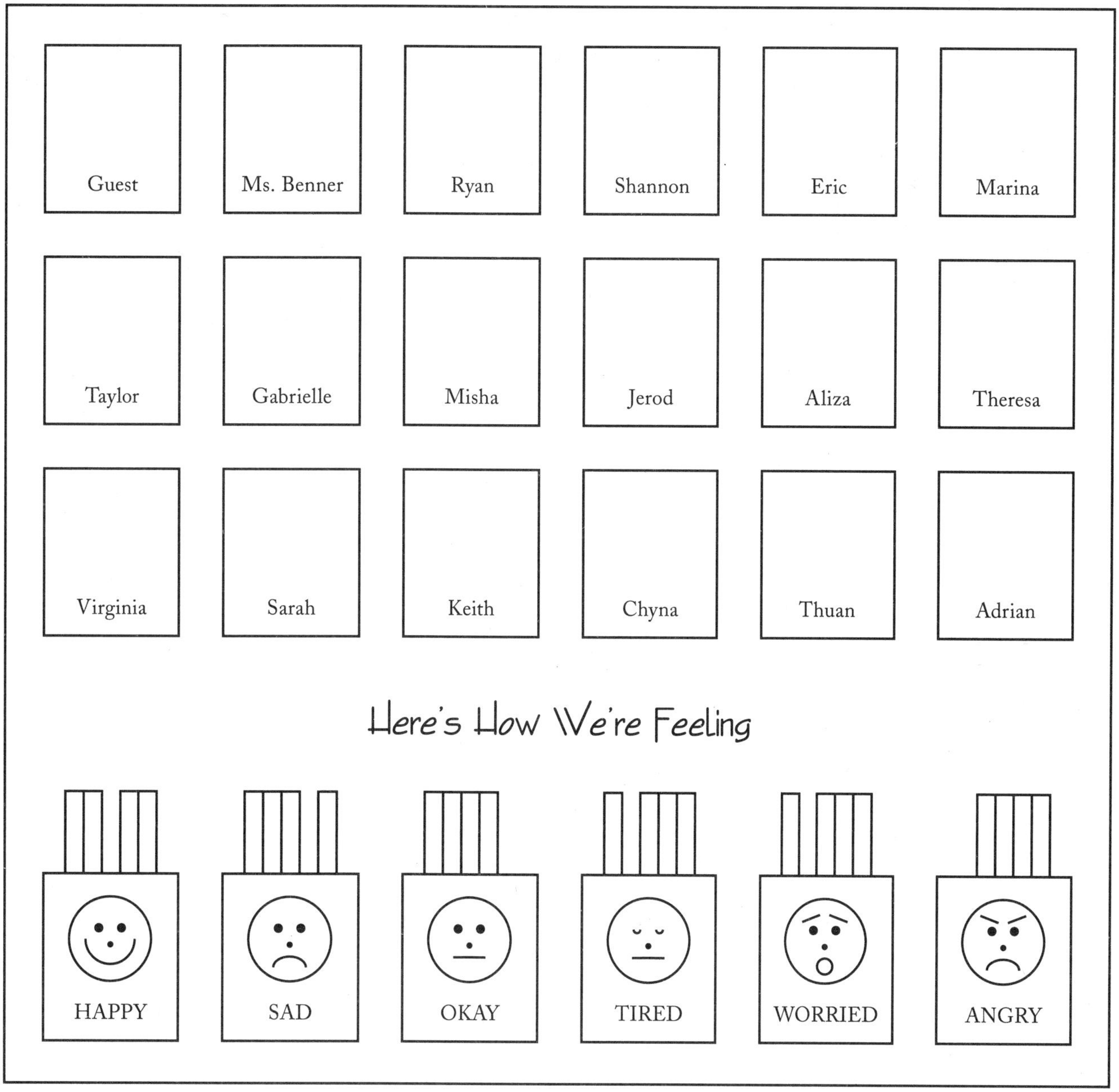

ings to others. You'll notice that the children tend to approach each other to ask about their feelings. It isn't necessary to take the time to discuss the children's feelings with the whole group. At times, you may want to seek out individual children to see if they need to talk.

Additional Resources

Butterworth, Nick. *Making Faces* (Candlewick Press, 1996). Discusses many different emotions and how people's faces look when they express them. Includes a mirror.

Preston, Edna Mitchell. *The Temper Tantrum Book* (Puffin Books, 1976). Baby animals have temper tantrums when things don't go their way. This book can lead to thoughtful discussions of other ways of dealing with anger.

Simon, Norma. *I Am* Not *a Crybaby* (Albert Whitman, 1989). Explores all of the situations in which crying is a natural and appropriate response.

LESSON 13

Speaking Up for Myself

People don't always know what others are thinking. Sometimes people have to speak up for themselves. We can help children learn to state their feelings, wishes, and needs in ways that show respect toward themselves and others.

Goals

1. To make children aware that one person may not always know what another person needs or wants.
2. To teach children an appropriate, respectful way to speak up for themselves.

Reading and Discussing the Poem

I'm a Person, Too

I'm not as big as you,
But I'm a person, too.
So treat me with respect,
And that's how I'll treat you.

Read the poem to the children and show the accompanying photograph. Ask questions like:

- "What is the child in the photograph doing?"
- "How do you feel when you're with people who are bigger or older than you? What kinds of things do they say to you?"
- "How do you feel when you're with people who are smaller or younger than you? What kinds of things do you say to them?"
- "What do you think the word *respect* means?"
- "Have you ever told someone that he or she wasn't treating you the way you want to be treated? What did you say?"

If you wish, explain the lesson theme: speaking up for myself. You might say, "Sometimes you need to tell other people how you feel and what you need. You need to *speak up for yourself.* You can do this in a way that shows *respect*—in a way that shows consideration and appreciation for others."

Activity: "I-Messages"

Materials needed:

- *Optional:* Chart paper and easel (or tape the paper to a chalkboard or wall); marker

Teach the children to use "I-messages" to tell someone else how they feel and what they want. Say something like, "Sometimes someone does something that we don't like. We need to tell the person how we feel. We need to explain what we want the person to do. We need to do this without calling the person a name. We need to do it without blaming the person.

"When we say '*You* make me angry' or '*You're* mean,' we're blaming the other person. That won't help the person want to respect us. It might make the person angry. It might turn things into a fight. A better way to tell the person how we feel is with an I-message. Instead of saying '*You,*' start by saying '*I.*'" Explain that the children can also use I-messages to tell the other person what they want.

Give the children examples of I-messages, such as:

- "I feel angry when you stay on the swing because I don't get a turn. I want you to give me a turn on the swing."

- "I feel sad when you call me names because it hurts my feelings. I want you to stop calling me names."
- "I feel upset when you talk because I can't hear the teacher. I want you to be quiet so I can hear."

Invite the children to suggest other I-messages. Guide them to find respectful words that don't label or blame.

If some of your students are able to read, you might want to make and display a poster of the I-message format for them to refer to:

I feel ________________________________

when ________________________________

because ______________________________.

I want you to__________________________.

Follow-up

Model the use of I-messages so the children become accustomed to hearing this assertive phrasing. Give positive reinforcement when you observe children respectfully speaking up for themselves. Really *listen* to the children, and foster a climate in which their appropriate attempts to get what they need are rewarded.

Additional Resources

Havill, Juanita. *Jamaica Tagalong* (Houghton Mifflin, 1980). When her older brother refuses to let her tag along with him, Jamaica allows a younger child to play with her.

Seuss, Dr. (Theodor Seuss Geisel). *Horton Hears a Who* (Random House, 1954). This delightful tale reinforces the message that we all need to make ourselves heard, because "a person's a person, no matter how small."

Zolotow, Charlotte. *I Like to Be Little* (HarperCollins, 1987). A little girl finds a way to explain that being little has its own rewards.

For adults: Dinkmeyer, Don Sr., et al. *The Parent's Handbook*, 3d rev. ed., and *Parenting Young Children*, 2d ed. (American Guidance Service, 1997). Based on *Systematic Training for Effective Parenting (STEP)*, these handbooks present step-by-step strategies, examples of I-messages, and other positive communication skills that are useful to parents and teachers alike.

LESSON 14

Understanding Others

It's important for people to care about one another. We can teach children to try to imagine what other people are experiencing and feeling. As we do this, we can guide children to use their understanding to find ways of showing that they care.

Goals

1. To help children think about and recognize how other people feel.
2. To emphasize the importance of showing others that we care about them.

Reading and Discussing the Poem

Someone Else's Chair

Want to learn about each other?
Want to show how much you care?
Just imagine what it's like
To sit in someone else's chair.

Show the children the photograph. Ask questions like:

- "What is one person in the picture doing for the other person?"
- "Can you tell about a time when you showed somebody that you cared? What did you do? Why did you do that?"

Point to the feet of the person pictured on the left and ask:

- "What kind of chair is this person sitting in? How can you tell?"
- "Do you know someone who uses a wheelchair? Have you ever been in a wheelchair? What do you think it would be like? What are some things you would do differently from the way you do them now?"

Read the poem to the children. Read it again and ask them to recite it along with you. They will probably be able to memorize it easily. Ask questions like:

- "What does it mean when the poem says 'imagine what it's like to sit in someone else's chair'?"
- "How do you feel when other people want to learn about you? Does it make you feel that they care about you?"
- "What are some ways you can learn about other people and their experiences?"

If you wish, explain the lesson theme: understanding others. You might say, "When we try to imagine how it feels to be like someone else, we're learning about *understanding others*."

Activities: 1. What Would It Be Like?

Explain to the children that you're going to tell them a brief story. Ask them to listen carefully and imagine how the people might be feeling. Say:

> Three children were playing together. They pretended they were firefighters. They polished the fire truck. They put on their hats and jackets. They wound the hoses and jumped on the truck. They drove the fire truck as fast as it would go. They made the siren wail.

Ask, "How do you think these children felt? Why do you think that?" Briefly discuss the children's responses. Then continue:

> There was a new child in school. The new child wanted to play, too. The new child stood nearby and watched the other children wind the hoses and drive the truck. The other kids were so busy playing that they didn't pay any attention to the new person at all.

Ask questions like:

- "How do you think the new child was feeling?"
- "Were the other children trying to be mean to the new person? Why do you think that?"
- "What are some ways the children could find out how the new child feels?"
- "What are some ways the children could show the new child that they care?"

Repeat the storytelling and discussion, using other situations your students will relate to. Each time, talk about the characters' feelings and the ways in which they could show that they care. Here are two suggested scenes:

- Some children make a mural with fingerpaints and leave a big mess. The custodian comes in to clean and finds the mess.
- A child has worked hard to make a model rocket. The child's friend accidentally drops the rocket and breaks it.

2. Sitting in Someone Else's Chair

Materials needed:

- Two chairs
- Index cards
- Marker
- Tape

Place the two chairs in front of the group. Choose one or more situations from the following chart, or use some of your own examples. Make labels and tape one to each chair:

Situation	***Chair 1 label***	***Chair 2 label***
Student chews gum in school	Student chewing gum	Custodian
Child plays with sister's or brother's toy without asking	Child playing with toy	Brother/sister
Child wants to stay up late to watch TV	Child	Parent

Ask two children to sit in the chairs. Explain that each child is to talk about the situation from the point of view of the person named on the chair. After each child has stated the person's point of view, ask the two students to switch chairs and state the other person's point of view.

Following each exchange, discuss with the group why people see things differently and have different opinions. Ask questions like:

- "Why did the student and the custodian have different opinions about chewing gum in school?"
- "Why did the brother and sister think differently about using the toy?"
- "Why did the parent and the child have different ideas about how late the child should stay up?"
- "How can people let each other know why they think the way they do?"

Follow-up

Encourage the children to stop and think about what another person might be experiencing. When reading stories, pause and ask questions about how the different story characters might feel. When children quarrel, remind them to look at the situation from each other's point of view. When talking to a child who has misbehaved, ask the child, "How would you like it if someone did that to you?" Help the child to role-play situations in order to experience the behavior from someone else's point of view.

Additional Resources

Carlson, Nancy. *Arnie and the New Kid* (Puffin Books, 1992). After he finds himself temporarily using crutches, Arnie learns to understand and be kinder to a classmate who uses a wheelchair.

Fox, Mem. *Wilfrid Gordon McDonald Partridge* (Kane/Miller, 1985). A little boy develops a special relationship with an elderly woman and helps her to "find" her lost memory.

Mandelbaum, Pili. *You Be Me and I'll Be You* (Kane/Miller, 1990). A young girl and her father who live in a biracial family talk about what it would be like to be each other.

Spinelli, Eileen. *Somebody Loves You, Mr. Hatch* (Simon & Schuster Books for Young Readers, 1991). A lonely, unsociable man changes his outlook when he receives an anonymous gift. After he discovers that the gift was meant for someone else, everyone in town joins together to let him know they care about him.

LESSON 15

Helping Others

None of us can function alone in the world. At various times we need help from others, and others need help from us. We can guide children to understand the importance of helping others. We can also show them that when they help another person, they feel good about themselves.

Goals

1. To make children aware that everyone needs help at times.
2. To demonstrate that it feels good to help someone else.
3. To encourage children to be helpful.

Reading and Discussing the Poem

I Don't Have the Time

I don't have the time.
I don't really care.

I don't want to do it.
I don't think it's fair.

I don't want to help you.
Can't you understand?

WHOOPS! I slipped!
Will you give me a hand?

Read all but the last two lines of the poem to the children. Ask questions like:

- "What are some of the reasons the person in the poem doesn't want to help someone else?"
- "How do you feel when you're really busy and somebody asks you for help?"
- "What are some of the ways that you're helpful?"

Then show the photograph to the children and read the last two lines of the poem. Ask questions like:

- "What does it mean when the person says, 'Will you give me a hand?'"
- "Why do you think the person is asking for help?"
- "Do you think the person will have a different feeling about helping others after being helped by someone else?"

If you wish, explain the lesson theme: helping others. You might say, "We all need help sometimes. We all need to *give* help sometimes, too. It feels good when someone helps you. *Helping others* feels good, too."

Activity: "Our Helping Hands" Bulletin Board

Materials needed:

- White 11″ × 17″ drawing paper
- Crayons, colored pencils, and/or markers

A day or two before doing this activity, begin to make a point of noticing when the children help one another; comment on it to the group. Say something like:

- "I see Yashira is helping Jackie learn her number facts."

- "I noticed that Alan helped Madison and Jee Sung water our plants."

Ask, "Has anyone else noticed someone helping?" Invite the children to tell about how individuals in the group have helped one another.

Tell the children that they can make a bulletin board showing some of the ways people in the group help each other. Distribute the drawing paper. On one section of the paper, have the children trace their hand and write or print their name inside of it. Ask the children to draw a "helping picture" next to the hand. Say, "You might draw a picture of yourself helping someone. You might draw a picture of someone else in our group helping you. Or you could draw a picture of someone in our group helping someone else."

Display the drawings on a bulletin board with the label, "Our Helping Hands."

Follow-up

1. Whenever you (or one of the children) notice people in the group spontaneously helping each other, write a sentence about it and add it to the bulletin board. Take photographs when you notice children helping one another. Add the photos to the bulletin board, too.
2. When a child asks you for help with a task, ask another child to help instead. For example, children can tie each other's shoes, help each other carry materials, or tell each other how to spell a word.
3. Provide opportunities for the children to help whenever they can. They can take responsibility for many of the jobs in the room, such as emptying the trash, passing out and collecting papers, filling in the calendar, or feeding pets. Be careful to avoid gender stereotyping when assigning jobs; encourage both girls and boys to help with all of the jobs.

Additional Resources

Bunting, Eve. *The Wednesday Surprise* (Clarion Books, 1989). As a surprise to the rest of the family, Anna helps her grandmother learn to read.

de Paola, Tomie. *Now One Foot, Now the Other* (G.P. Putnam's Sons, 1981). Bobby helps his grandfather to walk again following a stroke.

Galdone, Paul. *The Little Red Hen* (Clarion Books, 1973). None of the little red hen's animal friends are willing to help her do all that she needs to do in order to bake bread—but they all expect to be able to eat it!

Osofsky, Audrey. *My Buddy* (Henry Holt & Co., 1992). A young boy with muscular dystrophy is teamed up with a dog who helps him do things he's unable to do on his own.

LESSON 16

Cooperating

Children need to learn to work together in groups. We can use the expression "Two heads are better than one" to give children the message that a group of people working together can take advantage of everyone's skills, strengths, and talents.

★Goals

1. To teach children that cooperating can help everyone accomplish goals.
2. To make children aware that people's different skills and strengths can blend to enhance group projects.
3. To encourage children to work cooperatively with one another.

★Reading and Discussing the Poem

I Can't Move It

I can't move it,
You can't move it,
It won't move an inch.

But if we work together,
Moving it's a cinch.

Show the children the photograph. Ask questions like:

- "What are the girls in the photograph doing?"
- "Why do you think they are doing it together?"

Read the poem to the children. Read it again and ask them to recite it along with you. They will probably be able to memorize it easily. Ask questions like:

- "What are some things you can do with someone else that you probably couldn't do alone?"
- "What are some things you can think of that you would rather do without help?"
- "What are some things you might do at school that would be easier or better if you did them with other people?"

If you wish, explain the lesson theme: cooperating. You might say, "*Cooperating* can help us do things that are too hard for one person. When people work or play well together, they're cooperating. When people share ideas, they're cooperating."

★Activities: 1. Patchwork Quilt

Materials needed:

- 8½″ × 8½″ paper squares
- Crayons, markers, and/or colored pencils
- Art supplies: Paints, glitter, confetti, yarn, ribbon, wrapping paper, pipe cleaners, etc.
- Glue sticks
- Safety scissors
- Tape

Ask the children, "What is a patchwork quilt? Can you describe a patchwork quilt that you've seen?"

Discuss the idea that a patchwork quilt is made of individual pieces of cloth. Alone they are merely pretty patches; when put together, they turn into a beautiful quilt. Then say something like, "Our group can make our own patchwork quilt out of paper. Each of us can make one patch. Then we can put the patches together into a quilt that shows something about each of us and something about all of us together."

Have the children design, color, or decorate their square patches. Make your own patch, too. When everyone has finished, tape the squares together in a quilt pattern and display the quilt on a wall or bulletin board.

2. "Safe on the Island" Game

Materials needed:

- Masking tape or string
- Cassette or CD player
- Recorded music for movement

Using masking tape or string, mark off several 3′ × 3′ "islands" (about one island for every two or three children in your group) on the ground outside or on the floor inside.

Explain the game to the children by saying something like, "Who knows the game 'Musical Chairs'? We're going to play a game that works something like 'Musical Chairs.' Our game is called 'Safe on the Island.' When the music plays, you can swim around out here in the ocean." *(indicate the space around the islands)* "When the music stops, that means a storm is coming—all of you must get to an island in order to be safe from the storm! Remember, the group's goal is to keep everyone safe. More than one person can be on an island together. You don't want to leave anyone swimming in the storm."

Play the music and have the children swim for 15–20 seconds. Then stop the music and call out, "Storm's coming! Everybody swim to an island!" After everyone finds an island, play the music again. While the children swim, remove one island's masking tape or string. The children will have to cooperate as they make more room on the remaining islands to accommodate more people.

Continue playing and eliminating islands. Remind the children, "Remember to cooperate. Everyone needs to be safe!" Eventually, leave only two or three islands. The children will have to make adjustments in their use of the space so everyone can survive.

Follow-up

1. Allow children to work in pairs, rather than individually, as often as possible. They can divide tasks, do them together, or each do a portion of a single task. Give the children frequent opportunities to work on group projects such as posters, murals, or dioramas.
2. Play games in which the group has to cooperate to win. For example:
   - Instead of having the children compete for points, add each person's score to a group score. Give a group reward when a predetermined total is achieved.
   - Keep a puzzle going at all times. The number of pieces should depend on the ability level of the group. During free time, encourage the children to work on the puzzle alone and in small groups. They'll experience the challenge and fun of working on the puzzle and realize the value of cooperating to solve it.

Additional Resources

Lionni, Leo. *Swimmy* (Alfred A. Knopf, 1993). Swimmy teaches the other fish how to cooperate so they can scare away the big fish.

Rathmann, Peggy. *Officer Buckle and Gloria* (G.P. Putnam's Sons, 1995). This Caldecott Award winner tells the humorous story of how a safety officer and his dog work together to present school assemblies.

Sobel, Jeffrey. *Everybody Wins: 393 Non-Competitive Games for Young Children* (Walker & Co., 1983). All of the fun games described in this book stress participants' playing *with* rather than *against* each other.

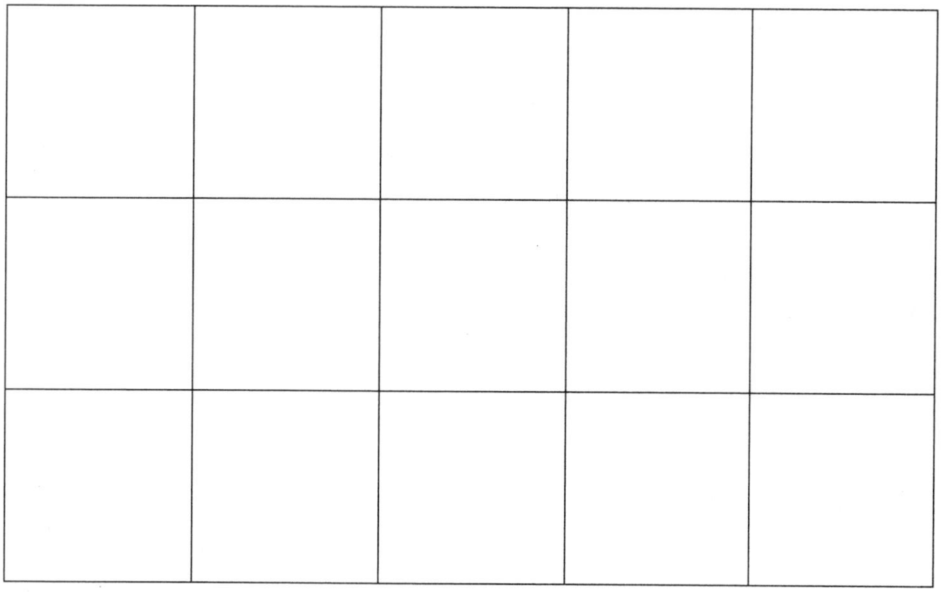

Sample layout for 15-patch quilt

Sample layout for 17-patch quilt

LESSON 17

Making Choices

Children need to know that they can choose to reach out to others to show that they care. We can help them ask and answer the question, "What is the best choice for me to make?" We can teach them the skills of decision making and give them practice in making choices.

Goals

1. To introduce the concept of personal choice.
2. To encourage children to look at many options and possible consequences when making choices.
3. To help children see that they can choose peaceful actions instead of fighting.

Reading and Discussing the Poem

Hands

Hands can fight,
Hands can scare,
Or hands can join together
To show they care.

Read the poem to the group and show the accompanying photograph. Ask questions like:

- "Whom do you think the hands in the photograph belong to? Do you think the people are friends? Why?"
- "Do you have a choice about what you do with your hands? What happens when people use their hands to fight and scare? What happens when people use their hands to show they care?"
- "If you're angry or don't agree with somebody, what are some things you can do instead of fight?"

This poem lends itself naturally to a finger play. Sit with the children in a circle and have them perform the motions as they recite each line with you:

Hands can fight,
(hold each hand in a tight fist)
Hands can scare,
(open the fists and spread hands outward in a scary motion)
Or hands can join together
To show they care.
(join hands with the people on each side of you)

If you wish, explain the lesson theme: making choices. You might say, "People don't have to fight. Each of us can *choose* to fight with other people *or* to use peaceful actions. We can make many kinds of choices, and each choice we make can bring different results."

Activity: Puppet Plays

Materials needed:

- Hand or stick puppets

Explain to the children that they will have a chance to create and present short puppet plays about choosing to work together to solve problems. With the whole group, talk briefly about problems the children might face and about possible ways to solve the problems. Ask questions like:

- "What is a problem that might happen on the playground? What are some ways you could choose to solve that problem?"

- "What is a problem that might happen during lunchtime? What are some ways you could choose to solve that problem?"
- "What is a problem that might happen with friends? With sisters and brothers? What are some ways you could choose to solve that problem?"

Divide the children into groups of two to four and explain the activity. Say something like, "We've just talked about some problems that can happen. Now you can make up puppet plays about solving problems. In your groups, decide on a problem you'd like to act out with puppets. The problem might be one we just talked about, but it doesn't have to be. Talk together about a problem. Discuss some possible ways to solve the problem and what could happen if you solve it each way. Choose a good way to solve the problem. Then practice your puppet play together."

Remind groups that each story should include a problem and a solution. Allow time for groups to plan and practice their puppet plays. Circulate and offer help as needed. The problems can be simple or more complex, depending on the age of the children.

Have groups present their puppet plays to the class. After each presentation, ask questions like:

- "What was the problem?"
- "Did the characters solve the problem? If they did, how did they decide to solve it? If they didn't, why weren't they able to solve it?"
- "How else might the characters have chosen to solve their problem?"

Follow-up

Notice and praise children when you observe them choosing to get along and to show others that they care. Empower the children by providing many opportunities for them to make choices that affect both their relationships with others and their everyday activities. Examples:

- "Shall we choose teams by counting off or by drawing straws?"
- "Shall we start with the poetry lesson or the art lesson?"

Sometimes it can take longer to allow the children to make choices than to tell them what to do, but the time you invest will pay off as they become more confident and adept at making good choices.

Additional Resources

Brott, Ardyth. *Jeremy's Decision* (Kane/Miller, 1997). A young boy is expected to follow in his father's footsteps and become an orchestra conductor, but he prefers to make a different choice.

Havill, Juanita. *Jamaica's Find* (Houghton Mifflin, 1986). Jamaica finds a stuffed dog on the playground and has to decide whether to seek out the owner or keep it.

Waber, Bernard. *Ira Sleeps Over* (Houghton Mifflin, 1972). A young boy struggles with the decision of whether to bring his teddy bear to a sleepover.

For adults: Simon, Sidney, Howard Kirschenbaum, and Leland Howe. *Values Clarification* (Warner Books, 1995). The 79 activities in this easy-to-use handbook give children practice in making decisions.

LESSON 18

Sharing

In order to share, children sometimes have to "give up" some of what they have. Yet, as they share with someone else, they'll often enjoy what they have even more. We can teach children the importance and the mutual benefits of sharing.

Goals

1. To emphasize the importance of sharing.
2. To help children recognize that sharing makes them feel good.
3. To demonstrate to children that the more they share with others, the more others are likely to want to share with them.

Reading and Discussing the Poem

Someone Who Knows How to Share

If one of us needs an eraser,
An eraser will be there,
Because it's fun
To be someone
Who knows how to share.

If one of use loses a pencil,
Another one will be there,
Because it's fun
To be someone
Who knows how to share.

And whenever we do something special,
We do it as a pair,
Because it's fun
To be someone
Who knows how to share.

Read the poem to the children and show the accompanying photograph. Ask questions like:

- "How are the girls in the photograph sharing?"
- "Can you think of a time when you shared with someone else? How did you feel?"
- "Can you think of a time when someone shared with you? How did you feel?"
- "Can you think of a time when someone wouldn't share with you? Why do you think the person wouldn't share? How did you feel?"

If you wish, explain the lesson theme: sharing. You might say, "*Sharing* can seem hard to do. But often it's more fun to share than it is to play alone. Sharing shows we care about other people."

Activity: Sharing Pairs

Materials needed:

- One small package of raisins or pretzels for each pair of children

Divide the children into pairs. Give each pair a small package of raisins or pretzels. Say, "You may share the treat. How you decide to do it is up to you."

After the children have had a few minutes to share their treat, gather the whole group together and ask each pair to tell the group how they shared it. Some responses might be:

- We counted them out—one for Noah, one for me.
- We each took a bunch, counted to make sure we had the same amount, and then made a change if we didn't.

Emphasize that sharing lets both people enjoy the treat.

Follow-up

1. Notice and point out when children are sharing. Occasionally distribute materials in a way that requires students to share. For example, give one set of watercolors or one set of math manipulatives to every two children.
2. Provide opportunities for the children to share their talents and skills, such as reading to younger children or making cards for residents in a nursing home.

Additional Resources

Lionni, Leo. *It's Mine!* (Alfred A. Knopf, 1985). Three frogs argue over who owns their pond and island, until a storm helps them realize the benefits of sharing.

Pfister, Marcus. *Rainbow Fish* (North-South Books, 1992). Rainbow Fish learns to share his shiny scales and gains friends in the process.

Wood, Don, and Audrey Wood. *The Little Mouse, the Red Ripe Strawberry, and the Big Hungry Bear* (Child's Play International Ltd., 1984). A little mouse has a strawberry that he tries to keep away from the big hungry bear. The mouse realizes the best way to protect the strawberry is to cut it in half and share it.

LESSON 19

Being a Friend

We all need friends. As children grow and begin to play with other children, we can help them learn the importance of friendship and the qualities that people value in a friend.

Goals

1. To emphasize that friends enjoy being together.
2. To make children aware that friends accept each other.
3. To help children see that to have a friend, one needs to be a friend.
4. To build children's understanding and awareness of the qualities of friendship.

Reading and Discussing the Poem

I Hope You're As Lucky As I Am

I hope you have someone to play with,
Someone who cares what you say.
I hope you are always together—
Even if one goes away.

I hope you can share all your feelings,
I hope you don't have to pretend.
I hope you're as lucky as I am—
I hope someone calls you a friend.

Read the title of the poem to the children. Ask, "Why do you think the person in the poem feels lucky?"

After hearing various responses, show the photograph to the children. Ask, "Do you have any other ideas about why the person feels lucky?"

Read the poem to the children. Ask questions like:

- "What are some ways the poem says that people can be friends?"
- "How can friends be together, even if one goes away?"
- "Do you share your feelings with your friends?"
- "Do you act like yourself when you're with your friends? Or do you try to act some other way, or 'pretend,' like it says in the poem?"
- "Do you feel lucky for the same reasons as the person in the poem? Why or why not?"

If you wish, explain the lesson theme: being a friend. You might say, "The poem is about *being a friend*. What does it mean to be a friend?"

Activities: 1. "This Is the Way to Be a Friend" Song

This activity uses the melody and rhythm to "Here We Go 'Round the Mulberry Bush."

Ask the children to name one way to be a friend (example: by sharing things together). Explain that you have a song everyone can sing about the ways to be a friend. Teach the song, using the way to be a friend you just discussed:

> This is the way to be a friend, be a friend, be a friend,
> This is the way to be a friend: *By sharing things together.*

Invite the children to suggest other ways to be a friend. Use each way to create and sing another verse to the song. It might be fun to pantomime the actions as you sing the song. It's not necessary for the words to rhyme or for the meter to be perfect. The goal is to have the children name and sing about as many qualities of a friend as possible. Some ending lines might be:

- By playing games together.
- By trying to understand.
- By showing that I care.
- By listening carefully.
- By telling how I feel.
- By asking how you feel.

2. Secret Pals for a Day

Materials needed:

- Slips of paper printed with individual children's names
- Hat

Put everyone's name in a hat. Tell the children that you're going to ask them to draw the name of a "secret pal" from the hat. Say, "Don't tell anyone whose name you draw. You want to be a *secret* friend to that person. You can do nice things for him or her. Part of the fun will be not knowing who your secret pal is."

Explain to the children that they can do thoughtful things for their pals today. Encourage students to try to find out as much as they can about their secret pals. The more they know, the more meaningful their friendly efforts will be. Give examples of things the children can do for their secret pals, such as:

- Make a point of sharing toys with your pal.
- Sharpen your pal's pencil.
- Draw pictures for or write notes to your pal.
- Try to cheer up a pal who looks lonely or sad.
- Give a red crayon to a pal who loves red.
- Cut a picture from a magazine of your pal's favorite sports player.
- If your pal loves puzzles, offer to work on one together.

At the end of the day, arrange a special time to disclose the identities of the pals. Some children may already have a good idea of who their pal is. Invite them to guess. Make sure everyone finds her or his secret pal. Encourage the children to thank their pals for their friendship.

Follow-up

1. Change seating, groups, and teams often. Regularly group the children in different ways and have them learn things about each other.
2. Tell the children about your own friends and why they're important to you.
3. With the children, do a group acrostic about the qualities of a friend. Here's one example:

F air
R eady to help
I nterested
E specially nice
N ever mean
D oes fun things

Additional Resources

Aliki. *We Are Best Friends* (Mulberry Books, 1987). When Robert's best friend moves away, both children are unhappy, but they learn that they can make new friends and still remain best friends.

Kellogg, Steven. *Best Friends* (Dial Books for Young Readers, 1986). This witty and imaginative story deals with the anger, jealousy, and other emotions that sometimes accompany friendship.

Viorst, Judith. *Rosie and Michael* (Aladdin Paperbacks, 1988). Rosie and Michael are the best of friends who like even the bad things about each other. They know they can always depend on one another.

LESSON 20

Getting Along

Children often argue because they want to do things their own way. It's important to teach children that they can get along better and accomplish more if they're willing to listen to other people's ideas. They can also learn to compromise or to come up with entirely new ideas together.

Goals

1. To help children see that someone else can have good ideas that might be different from their own.
2. To teach the concept of compromising as a way to get along with others.
3. To encourage children to compromise in order to get along.

Reading and Discussing the Poem

Five Little People

Five little people went out to play.

The first one said, "Do it my way!"
The second one said, "That's not fair!"
The third one said, "I don't care!"
The fourth one said, "This isn't fun!"
The fifth one said, "Our game is done!"

So five little people all walked away.
They never even got to play.

Show the children the photograph. Ask questions like:

- "What do you think is happening in the picture?"
- "Why do you think the children are walking in different directions?"
- "If you were one of the children, what would you do next?"

Read the poem to the children. Read it again and ask them to recite it along with you. After a few repetitions, the children will probably memorize the poem. Ask questions like:

- "Why do you think the children in the poem didn't get to play?"
- "What could they have done differently?"
- "Can you remember a time when you didn't get to play because you and your friends spent too much time arguing? Tell us what happened. What could you do differently next time?"

Read the poem again and demonstrate it as a finger play:

Five little people went out to play.
(hold up one hand, spread out all five fingers)

The first one said, "Do it my way!"
(close fist, then hold up index finger only)
The second one said, "That's not fair!"
(keeping index finger up, hold up middle finger as well)
The third one said, "I don't care!"
(add next finger to others held up)
The fourth one said, "This isn't fun!"
(add pinkie)
The fifth one said, "Our game is done!"
(add thumb; now all five fingers are held up)

So five little people all walked away.
They never even got to play.
(turn hand upside down and "walk" with your fingers)

If you wish, explain the lesson theme: getting along. You might say, "The people in the poem were having trouble *getting along*. If people want to do things only *their* way, it can be hard to get along."

Activity: Group Collages

Materials needed:

- Posterboard, chart paper, or 11″ × 17″ sheets of construction paper
- Magazines
- Safety scissors
- Glue sticks
- Crayons, colored pencils, and/or markers

In this activity, the children will gain experience in listening, expressing their opinions, brainstorming, discovering commonalities, and compromising.

Divide the children into groups of three or four. Tell them that each group is going to work together to make a collage. Ask them to think about the kinds of pictures they want to put in their collage. Ask questions like:

- "What kinds of pictures do *you* want to use?"
- "What kinds of pictures do you think someone else in your group wants to use? How can you find out?"
- "How can you make a collage that everyone in your group will feel happy about?"

Stress that everyone in the group will need to work to get along. Help the children recognize that they need to ask and then listen to each person's ideas. Remind them that they can all have fun by planning and make a collage that they can all agree about.

Invite the children to brainstorm ideas about the collage. You might want to make suggestions like:

- "If Tycel has an idea, he can tell Wendy and Jason his idea, and they can listen to Tycel."
- "Maybe Nate and Suzy can cut out pictures and T.J. can glue them to the paper."
- "If Saundra wants to use sports pictures and Juana and Michael want to show nature scenes, maybe the group can look for people doing outdoor sports like mountain climbing or skiing."

Distribute the art materials. Give the groups time to plan and make their collages. If groups get stuck, or seem headed toward a conflict, remind them of the children in the poem and how they needed to get along in order to have fun together.

Display the collages and invite groups to tell about how they were able to get along in order to create them.

Follow-up

Praise the children when you observe them listening to each other's ideas and compromising. On days when the children have accomplished all their tasks without squabbling, allow a bit of extra playtime at the end of the day. Tell students, "You didn't waste time arguing today, so you have time left over for fun!"

Additional Resources

Ernst, Lisa Campbell. *Zinnia and Dot* (Puffin Books, 1992). Two hens are so involved in fighting over who owns the eggs that they destroy all but one. Together, they must come up with a plan to save the last egg.

Lalli, Judy. *Make Someone Smile and 40 More Ways to Be a Peaceful Person* (Free Spirit Publishing Inc., 1996). This book combines simple words with black-and-white photographs by Douglas L. Mason-Fry to offer suggestions for how to interact successfully, cooperatively, and peacefully with others.

Lionni, Leo. *Six Crows* (Alfred A. Knopf, 1988). An owl helps a farmer and some crows to reach a compromise over the rights to the wheat crop.

Payne, Lauren Murphy, and Claudia Rohling. *We Can Get Along: A Child's Book of Choices* and *A Leader's Guide to We Can Get Along* (Free Spirit Publishing Inc., 1997). The simple text and appealing illustrations of the children's book strengthen and support children in choosing actions that help them get along with others. The companion Leader's Guide contains lessons, follow-up questions, reading lists, and reproducibles for teachers and parents.

For adults: Kreidler, William. *Creative Conflict Resolution* (Scott, Foresman & Co., 1984). This resource book offers over 200 classroom-tested activities and cooperative games to help children improve communication and resolve conflicts.

LESSON 21

Doing It Ourselves

Self-sufficiency is a valuable life skill. The more capable children feel, the better they'll feel about themselves. In our well-meaning attempts to help children, we sometimes step in too soon. We can help children become more self-sufficient by encouraging them to do as much as possible for themselves.

★Goals

1. To make children aware that there are many things they can do on their own.
2. To encourage children to do as much for themselves as possible.
3. To help children feel more capable by providing opportunities for them to do things on their own.

★Reading and Discussing the Poem

We're Telling the Teacher on You

"We're telling the teacher on you!"
"We're telling the teacher on you!"

Wait a minute! That's not fair!
The teacher wasn't even there.

She won't know what it's about,
So let's sit down and work it out.

Read the poem to the children a few times, exaggerating the whiny, "tattle-tale" words. Show the accompanying photograph. Ask questions like:

- "What do you think the children in the poem wanted to tell the teacher?"
- "Do you think it might be better for the children to work it out themselves? Why?"
- "How could they work it out?"
- "Think of a time when you were able to do something on your own. How did you feel?"
- "How can you decide if you should tell the teacher something?"

During the discussion, emphasize the difference between minor disputes involving things like name-calling and major problems involving health and safety issues, such as fighting.

Children enjoy reciting this poem and "playing the parts." Divide the children into two groups, and have one group recite the first stanza and the other respond with the second and third stanzas. Then switch groups so everyone has a turn reciting both parts of the poem.

If you wish, explain the lesson theme: doing it ourselves. You might say, "The poem is about *doing things for ourselves*. There are lots of times when you can work out problems on your own, without a teacher or parent."

★Activities: 1. "Do-It-Ourselves" List

Materials needed:

- Chart paper and easel (or tape the paper to a chalkboard or wall)
- Marker

Along with the children, create a list of jobs and tasks that the children can do by themselves. Some examples of the items on the list, depending on your particular environment, might be:

- sharpening my pencil
- taping my ripped paper

- keeping my desk clean
- getting my own materials for a project and returning them to the proper place
- resolving a conflict with someone.

2. Peace Place*

Materials needed:

- Copy of the "Rules of the Peace Place" on page 56

Set up a "Peace Place" in the room with the "Rules of the Peace Place" clearly displayed. Explain to the children that this is where they can go if they need to resolve a conflict. Talk about some situations they could resolve in the "Peace Place," such as:

- name-calling
- not allowing someone to play a game
- borrowing someone's pencil and not returning it.

Teach the children the "Rules of the Peace Place":

1. Go to the "Peace Place" if someone asks you to.
2. Use respectful words.
3. Take turns speaking and listening to each other.
4. Use I-messages. (Example: "I get angry when you take my pencil without asking because then I don't have a pencil to use. I want you to ask me first." See Lesson 13, pages 36–37, for a detailed explanation of I-messages.)
5. If the problem is too big for you to solve, get help from a grownup.

The "Peace Place" saves time by cutting down on tattling. It provides opportunities for the children to resolve their own conflicts, many of which are based on misunderstandings.

Follow-up

1. With the children, add to the "Do-It-Ourselves" list throughout the year. It will be a visual reminder of self-reliance and a great confidence builder.
2. Empower the children by allowing them to do as much as they can by themselves, whenever possible. Help them to be less dependent on you by teaching them the phrase, "Ask three before me." Tell them that before automatically turning to the teacher for answers to their questions, they should ask up to three other children for help. Some situations in which this would be appropriate would be tying shoes, clarifying directions, spelling a word, or finding a particular page in a book. Over time, this strategy has the potential to lead to more efficient use of your time and resources, increased student responsibility, and improved group interactions. An added bonus is that the children often become better able to explain directions and to do things in ways that their peers understand.
3. Trust the "Peace Place" process. When you let the children resolve problems on their own, they may not come up with the result you might have preferred or predicted. Remember, the important thing is that you are giving the children practice in working things out themselves. Be available, however, and step in when you feel you need to.
4. Copy the Home Handout for this lesson, "20 Ways to Help Your Child Get Along with Others," to send home to parents or caregivers.

Additional Resources

Bingham, Mindy. *Minou* (Advocacy Press, 1987). A cat who doesn't know how to take care of herself learns the skills of self-reliance after being abandoned in the streets of Paris.

Johnston, Tony. *Amber on the Mountain* (Dial Books for Young Readers, 1994). Anna teachers Amber how to read; then Amber teaches herself how to write.

Saltzman, David. *The Jester Has Lost His Jingle* (The Jester Company, 1996). This uplifting tale of a jester who searches the world for happiness and then finds it within himself is particularly poignant because it was written by a young man who knew he was dying at the time he wrote it.

Zolotow, Charlotte. *The Hating Book* (Harper & Row, 1969). A little girl feels that she hates a friend who snubs her, but eventually works the problem out with the friend.

* This activity was developed by Judy Lalli and Diane O'Neill, teacher, Paul V. Fly Elementary School, Norristown, PA. Used with permission of Diane O'Neill.

Rules of the Peace Place

1. Go to the "Peace Place" if someone asks you to.

2. Use respectful words.

3. Take turns speaking and listening to each other.

4. Use I-messages:

I feel ______________________________

when ______________________________

because ______________________________ .

I want you to ________________________ .

5. If the problem is too big for you to solve, get help from a grownup.

20 Ways to Help Your Child Get Along with Others

1. Treat your child with kindness and respect.
2. Build your child's self-esteem. It's hard to show respect to others when you don't feel good about yourself.

   Say: *"You can do it," "I appreciated that,"* and *"You're a wonderful kid!"*

   Ask: *"How do you do that?"* and *"Can you please teach me that?"*
3. Let your child know that everyone has feelings and that feelings are okay. Teach your child words for feelings.
4. Remind your child to think about how others feel.
5. Say "please" and "thank you" to your child. Teach your child that manners are important, even with people we see every day.
6. Encourage your child to do caring things for others. Let your child see you doing caring things for others.
7. Teach your child not to tease or call people names.
8. Use I-messages to state your feelings respectfully. Avoid you-messages, which blame or criticize. For example, instead of saying "Why do you always whine when it's time for bed?" try this:

   "I feel frustrated when I hear whining about bedtime because it wastes time that we could be enjoying together. I want you to get ready for bed quietly."
9. Encourage your child to use I-messages instead of you-messages. (See #20.)
10. Praise your child for using respectful words.
11. Try to let your child solve some problems on his/her own.
12. Teach your child that hitting, pushing, biting, kicking, and other violent actions are *not* okay.

➜

13. Model peaceful conflict resolution in your home.
14. Take the time to sit down and talk about small conflicts before they become big problems.
15. Teach the art of compromise.
16. Teach your child that sometimes people can agree to disagree.
17. Praise your child for trying to resolve conflicts peacefully.
18. Smile and be friendly toward others.
19. Encourage your child to say "I'm sorry" when she/he has done something that negatively affects someone else.
20. Have a "Peace Place" in a room or corner of your home. Post these rules:

1. Go to the "Peace Place" if someone asks you to.
2. Use respectful words.
3. Take turns speaking and listening to each other.
4. Use I-messages:

   I feel ______________________________

   when ______________________________

   because ____________________________.

   I want you to ________________________.

LESSON 22

Being Polite

Manners are important for any group of people. We teach even very young children polite words, such as "please" and "thank you," and polite behaviors, such as taking turns. As children grow older, we need to remind them to continue using manners. We also need to help children understand why courtesy is important.

Goals

1. To remind children of simple words and behaviors that demonstrate good manners.
2. To help children understand how manners make it easier for people to get along.
3. To encourage children to be polite.

Reading and Discussing the Poem

I Forgot to Say "Please" and "Thank You"

I forgot to say "Please" and "Thank you."
I forgot to take turns with the ball.
I forgot to say "May I?" and "Sorry."
I forgot to use manners at all.

The other kids tried to remind me,
But I just forgot what to say.
Then they all forgot their manners—
They forgot to invite me to play.

Tell the children the title of the poem. Ask:

- "Why do you think the person forgot to say 'please' and 'thank you'?"
- "What else do you think the person forgot to do?"

Tell the children that the poem is about using manners, and that what the person forgot to do was to be polite. Read them the poem and show the accompanying photograph. Many students will have guessed that someone who doesn't use manners might not be invited to play. Ask questions like:

- "Why do you think the boy looks so sad?"
- "What do you think he learned?"
- "Do you use good manners with other people?"
- "Do you like it when people use good manners with you?"

If you wish, explain the lesson theme: being polite. You might say, "People like to be treated politely. *Being polite* helps people to get along."

Activity: "Magic Word" Wands

Materials needed:

- Drinking straws or unsharpened pencils
- Aluminum foil or foil wrapping paper
- Copies of the "Please/Thank You" handout on page 61 (best if copied on heavy paper)
- Safety scissors
- Crayons, colored pencils, and/or markers
- Tape

Introduce the term "magic words" and explain that good manners are like "magic" because when we use them, people are more likely to do what we want them to do. Ask questions like:

- "What are some 'magic words' that you use that show good manners?"
- "What are some ways you act that show good manners?"

Examples might include holding a door for someone, waiting for a turn at a water fountain without pushing, not speaking with a full mouth, and not interrupting people when they're talking.

Have the children make "Magic Word Wands" to help them remember the words "please" and "thank you." Wrap drinking straws or unsharpened pencils with aluminum foil or foil wrapping paper. Give each child a copy of the "Please/Thank You" handout. Read or have the children read the words aloud. Let the children color or decorate the word stars. Assist the children as needed to cut along the solid line. Fold on the dotted line. Tape the edges along the top. Tape the star securely to the end of the foil-covered stick.

Tell the children, "Your 'Magic Word Wand' can remind you to be polite to other people."

Follow-up

Let the children know that you expect them to use the "magic words." Praise the children when you hear or see them using good manners. Model being polite. Allow the children to observe you using good manners in your daily interactions.

Additional Resources

Aliki. *Manners* (Greenwillow Books, 1990). Many different manners are cleverly illustrated in this delightful book.

Austin, Virginia. *Say Please* (Candlewick Press, 1996). A little boy learns from his animal friends to say "please" and "thank you."

Brown, Marc, and Stephen Krensky. *Perfect Pigs: An Introduction to Manners* (Little, Brown & Co., 1983). Pigs are used to illustrate a variety of manners for children.

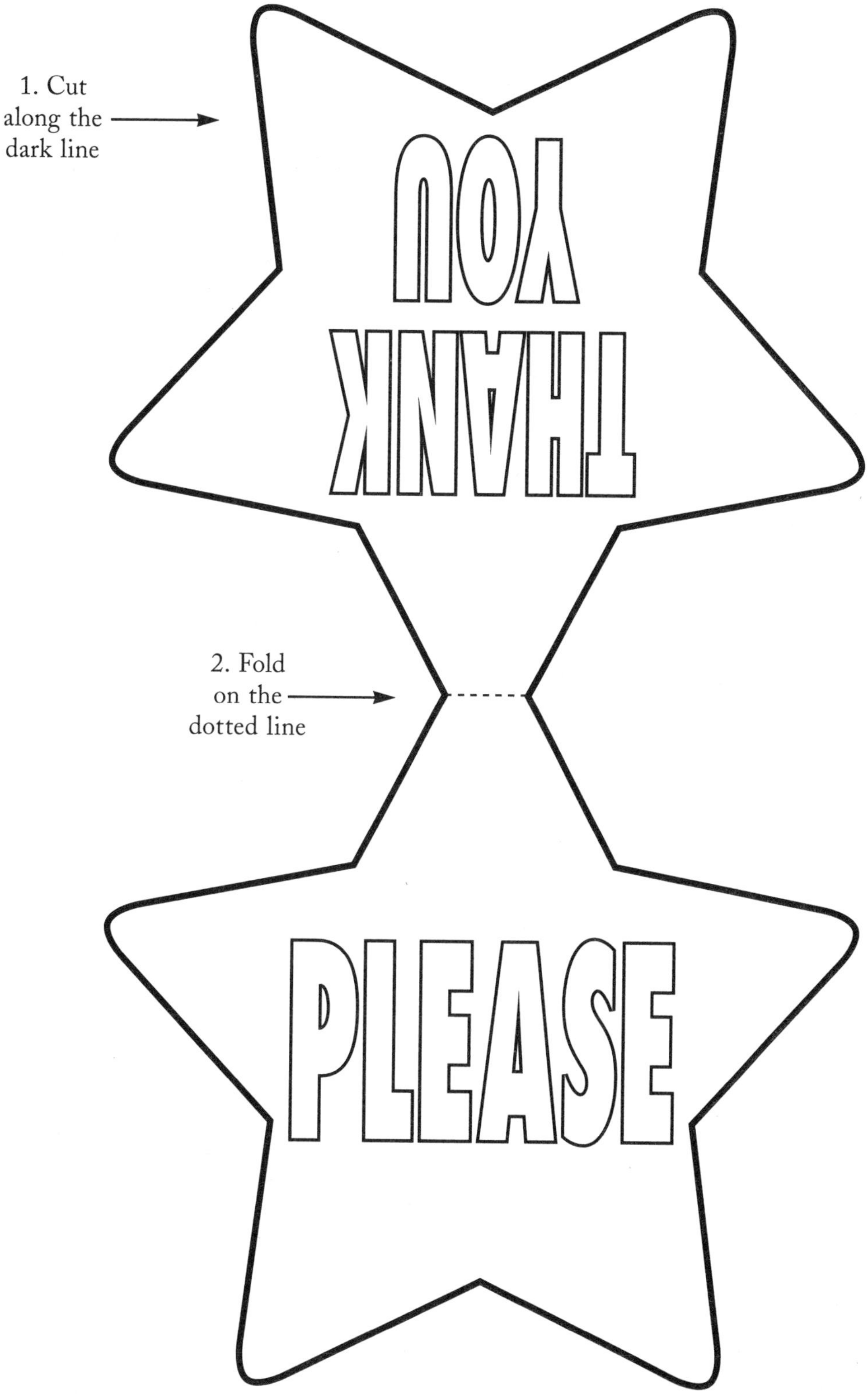
1. Cut along the dark line
THANK YOU
2. Fold on the dotted line
PLEASE

LESSON 23

Saying "I'm Sorry"

Adults often tell children, "Say you're sorry." It's important for children to learn to apologize and to understand why apologies are important, so that eventually they will offer sincere apologies instead of rote ones.

Goals

1. To remind children that it's important to apologize when they've done something that negatively affects someone else.
2. To introduce the idea that sincere apologies make people feel better.
3. To emphasize that the best apologies go hand-in-hand with a decision to act differently next time.
4. To help children become more willing to apologize.

Reading and Discussing the Poem

There Are Only Two Kinds of "I'm Sorry"

There are only two kinds of "I'm sorry,"
With no other kind in between.
There's the one that someone *tells* you
to say
And the one that you really mean.

Read the poem to the children and show the accompanying photograph. After hearing the poem a few times, the children should be able to recite it along with you. Ask questions like:

- "What are the two kinds of 'I'm sorry' in the poem?"
- "Has anyone ever told you to say you were sorry when you didn't want to say it? Why didn't you want to? What did you do? How did you feel?"
- "Have you ever said you were sorry without being told to? What happened? How did you feel?"
- "Do you think it's important to apologize? Why?"
- "When other people tell you they're sorry, how can you show them that you accept the apology?"

If you wish, explain the lesson theme: saying "I'm sorry." You might say, "The poem is about *saying 'I'm sorry'* and *meaning* it."

Activity: Sounds Like, Looks Like

Materials needed:

- Chart paper and easel (or tape the paper to a chalkboard or wall)
- Marker

Divide the chart paper vertically and horizontally to make a T-chart. At the top of the left-hand column, write the words "Sounds Like"; at the top of the right-hand column, write the words "Looks Like."

Point to the words at the top of the left-hand column and read them to the children. Then ask, "What does an apology *sound like*? What words do people use when they apologize?" Write the children's responses in the left-hand column of the chart. Children's ideas might include:

- "I'm sorry."
- "I promise I won't do it again."
- "It was my fault."
- "I didn't mean to."

Next, point to the words at the top of the right-hand column and read them to the children. Then ask, "What does an apology *look like*? What do people *do* to show they really mean that they're sorry?" Write the children's responses in the right-hand column of the chart. Children's ideas might include:

- Look at the person you're talking to.
- Help to solve the problem.
- Shake hands.
- Do something nice for the person.

Follow-up

1. Set up a role play. Have two children pretend to be building with blocks, and have another child pretend to accidentally knock the blocks over, apologizing after doing so. Ask the children to act out what might happen next. (Example: All three children rebuild what was knocked down.)
2. Refrain from demanding that children apologize in the heat of the moment, when they're not feeling sorry. Allow a cooling-off period. Once a child has apologized, validate the student for doing so. Guide the person receiving the apology to accept it without further comment. Encourage the children involved to solve any problems that were caused by their actions and to plan alternatives in order to avoid repeating the behavior.

Additional Resources

DePaolo, Paula. *Rosie and the Yellow Ribbon* (Little, Brown & Co., 1992). Rosie mistakenly blames her friend for the loss of a favorite ribbon and apologizes when she realizes her mistake.

Henkes, Kevin. *Lilly's Purple Plastic Purse* (Greenwillow Books, 1996). Lilly writes a mean note to her much-admired teacher and then is truly sorry, so she writes an apology from the heart.

Zolotow, Charlotte. *The Quarreling Book* (HarperCollins, 1991). A chain reaction of quarreling gets turned around, and everyone involved apologizes or does something kind.

LESSON 24

Caring About Our World

We know that we have limited resources on our planet. Recycling containers are a fact of life in many children's schools and homes. We need to help children realize that they play an important role in protecting our environment as they "Reduce, Reuse, and Recycle."

Goals

1. To encourage children to care about the environment.
2. To demonstrate ways to reduce waste by reusing and recycling things.
3. To build children's awareness of the responsibility we all have for taking care of our world.
4. To teach children to take care of their things so they will last.

Reading and Discussing the Poem

You Can Use It

You can use it,
Reuse it,
Recycle it, and then
You can use it,
Reuse it, and
Recycle it again.

Or. . .

You can use it,
Abuse it,
Throw it on the ground,
Till all you see is trash
When you look around.

Or. . .

You can use it,
Reuse it,
Recycle it, and then
You can use it,
Reuse it, and
Recycle it again.

Read the poem to the children and show the accompanying photograph. Ask questions like:

- "How do you think the children in the picture feel when they see trash on the ground?"
- "How do you feel when you see trash on the ground?"
- "What do you do when you're outside and you have trash to throw away? What if there's no trash can nearby?"

If you wish, explain the lesson theme: caring about our world. You might say, "The poem talks about *reusing* and *recycling*. These are ways that we *care about our world*."

Activity: Tree Art

Materials needed:

- Drawing paper that's been used on one side
- Crayons, colored pencils, and/or markers
- A variety of discarded papers intended for recycling
- Safety scissors
- Glue sticks

Discuss with the children the fact that paper comes from trees. Have them brainstorm all the ways they could conserve paper and thereby save trees. Some examples might be:

- Write on both sides of a paper.
- Take only one napkin or paper towel at a time.
- Carry a reusable bag instead of a paper bag for lunches and snacks.
- Recycle paper that can't be used again.

Involve the children in recycling paper by using discarded papers in an art project. Give the children used drawing paper and crayons, colored pencils, and/or markers. Ask them to draw the trunk and branches of a tree. Then have the children cut "leaves" from discarded paper, color them if they wish, and glue them to the tree branches.

Display the trees on the walls in your room or in the hallway.

Follow-up

Point out opportunities to use items completely before discarding them. For example, crayons can be used even after they're broken; pencils can be used even when they're quite short. Reduce waste and unnecessary recycling by keeping a scrap-paper box in the room. Papers used only slightly or on one side can often be reused for practice paper or art projects.

Additional Resources

Brown, Laurie Krasny, and Marc Brown. *Dinosaurs to the Rescue! A Guide to Protecting Our Planet* (Little, Brown & Co., 1992). The dinosaur characters in this book introduce children to the earth's major environmental problems and suggest ways children can begin to help solve them.

Gilman, Phoebe. *Something from Nothing* (Scholastic, 1992). A young Jewish boy learns from his grandfather how to preserve his favorite blanket by remaking it into many different things over the years.

Schimmel, Schim. *Dear Children of the Earth* (NorthWord Press, 1994). This beautifully illustrated book is a letter from Mother Earth to children asking them to love her, care for her, and protect her.

Udry, Janice. *A Tree Is Nice* (HarperCollins, 1984). All the wonderful things trees are used for, from holding a swing to providing shade, are illustrated in this book.

LESSON 25

Showing Appreciation

In November, many people in the United States celebrate the Thanksgiving holiday. It's a time to think about all that we appreciate. We can also take time throughout the rest of the year to acknowledge how grateful we are for what we have and for what others do for us. We can help children to recognize what they appreciate and to learn to say "thank you" to others.

Goals

1. To help children see that they have much to be thankful for.
2. To emphasize that it's important to show appreciation to others.

Reading and Discussing the Poem

We Give Thanks

We give thanks
In late November.

But what about January
February
March
April
May
June
July
August
September
October
and December?

The best time for Thanksgiving
Is every day we're living.

If you teach outside the United States, explain to the children that there is a day in the U.S. when Americans give thanks for food, families, friends, and a safe place to live. Other countries, including Canada, also have special Thanksgiving Days.

Ask the children:

- "What is Thanksgiving?"
- "When is Thanksgiving?"

If no one offers a response, say something like: "Thanksgiving is a day when people give thanks. It's in November." Elaborate as you see fit. Then say, "Here's a poem about all the other times of the year when we can be thankful."

Read the poem to the children and show the accompanying photograph. The children will probably want to repeat the poem with you, as they enjoy saying the months of the year. Ask questions like:

- "How do you think the children are feeling?"
- "What do you think they might be thankful for?"
- "What are you thankful for?"
- "How do you show when you're thankful?"

If you wish, explain the lesson theme: showing appreciation. You might say, "When we show that we're thankful, we *show appreciation*. What's *appreciation*? What does it mean to appreciate something?"

Activities: 1. Appreciation Circle

This quick activity gives children the opportunity to reflect on things that they're thankful for and to listen to what other people are thankful for as well.

Have the children sit in a circle. Explain that it's an "Appreciation Circle." Go around the circle and invite children to tell something they're thankful for.

NOTE: As with any sharing activity of this kind, be sure to include a "pass" option.

2. Thank-You Notes

Materials needed:

- Copies of the "Thank You" handout on page 68
- Safety scissors
- Crayons, colored pencils, and/or markers

Tell the children that they can write thank-you notes to someone they appreciate. Talk about whom they might thank and what they might say "thank you" for. Here are some ideas:

- Thank the custodian for keeping the room clean and providing supplies.
- Thank a parent who sent in treats or helped with a field trip.
- Thank a visitor who presented a special program to the group.
- Thank the bus or van driver for driving safely.

Give each child a copy of the "Thank You" handout. Read or have the children read the words aloud. Assist the children as needed to cut along the solid line and fold on the dotted line. Have the children decorate the "Thank You" side of the card. On the inside, suggest that they draw a picture and write or dictate sentences that tell why they appreciate the person. The recipients of the cards will be thrilled, and the children will enjoy making others feel appreciated.

Follow-up

Have the children sit in another "Appreciation Circle" and complete the sentence "I want to thank _____ (name of person) because _____ (reason)." Some examples might be:

- "I want to thank Carlos because he shared his crayons with me."
- "I want to thank Tiana because she helped me with my math."

Be aware of children who may be doing positive things and not getting recognized. You can always take a turn and offer your appreciation to them.

Repeat this exercise often. It doesn't take much time, and it lets the children know that good deeds do get noticed.

Additional Resources

Baylor, Byrd. *I'm in Charge of Celebrations* (Simon & Schuster, 1986). A young Native American girl creates her own celebrations as she appreciates the wonders of the desert wilderness around her.

Leedy, Loreen. *Messages in the Mailbox: How to Write a Letter* (Holiday House, 1991). This colorful book discusses different kinds of letters, including thank-you notes, and provides easy-to-follow examples.

Spinelli, Eileen. *Thanksgiving at the Tappletons'* (HarperTrophy, 1982). When their traditional Thanksgiving dinner is spoiled, the Tappletons realize that there is more to Thanksgiving than turkey and trimmings.

LESSON 25 HANDOUT

LESSON 26

Celebrating Differences

Our world is made up of many unique individuals who are different in many ways. These differences make our lives rich and interesting. We need to teach children not just to tolerate diversity, but to celebrate it.

Goals

1. To make children aware of some of their differences and similarities.
2. To help children recognize that people's differences make them interesting.
3. To help children learn about, respect, and appreciate each other's differences.

Reading and Discussing the Poem

Boring, Boring, Boring

Boring, boring, boring.
That's what my world would be
If everybody looked and talked
And acted just like me.

Read the poem to the children and then have them recite it with you. They will memorize it quickly and will especially enjoy exaggerating the sounds of the first three words.

Show the children the photograph. Ask questions like:

- "How are these children the same?"
- "How are these children different?"
- "What are the children doing in the picture?"
- "What does it mean to be *bored*? Do you agree that it would be boring if everybody was the same? Why or why not?"
- "Do you know people who look, talk, or act like you? Do you know people who look, talk, or act differently from you?"

If you wish, explain the lesson theme: celebrating differences. You might say, "Differences are interesting. They're fun. As we learn about how we're alike and different, we can *celebrate the differences*. What does it mean to *celebrate*? What are some ways we could celebrate being different?"

Activities: 1. Find Your Lemon

Materials needed:

- One lemon for each child in the group
- *Optional:* Large juice container and spoon for stirring, sharp knife (for the teacher), water, sugar, ice, drinking cups

This activity demonstrates dramatically that even in a group where everything seems very much the same, there can be uniqueness.

Have the children sit in a circle. Hold up a lemon. Ask:

- "How big is a lemon?"
- "What color is a lemon?"
- "What shape does a lemon have?"
- "Do you think most lemons look pretty much the same?"

Distribute a lemon to each child in the group. Tell the children to examine their lemon closely, observing its shape, bumps, special markings, stickers, blemishes, and stem. Say, "Look very closely, so you can find what's *unique* about your lemon—what makes it one of a kind."

Have the children place their lemons in the center of the circle. Mix up the lemons. Wait a few moments and then tell the children that you want them to find their own lemons. Depending on the number of children in the group and their age level, you can have them retrieve their lemons all at once or a few at a time. Most students will be able to find their own individual lemons!

Collect the lemons. Say, "You know that lemons are alike in many ways. You've learned that each lemon is also unique." Ask questions like:

- "What are some ways that all people are the same?"
- "What are some ways that people are different?"
- "How are you the same as everyone in this group?"
- "How are you unique?"

If you like, use the lemons to make lemonade. Point out that all of the different lemons contribute to making good lemonade, just as different individuals contribute something to the group.

2. We're Alike and Different

Have the children form two circles, one inside the other. The children can be standing or sitting. The people in the inner circle should face out; the people in the outer circle should face in. When each child is facing a partner, say, "You have one minute to talk to your partner and find out three things that are the same about you and three things that are different."

After the minute is up, ask the children in the outside circle to move one person to the right. The children will once again have a minute to talk to their new partners about their similarities and differences. Repeat this as time allows. Then ask the whole group:

- "What are some things you learned about each other?"
- "What are some ways you and your partners are alike?"
- "What are some ways you and your partners are different?"

Follow-up

1. Establish an atmosphere in which it's okay to be different. Not every child has to use the same color paper for a project, the same sequence for completing tasks, or the same method for finding a solution to a math problem. Let the children know that they can feel safe asking to do something in a new way.
2. Copy the Home Handout for this lesson, "Celebrating Differences: Books to Share with Your Child" to send home to parents or caregivers.

Additional Resources

Cannon, Janell. *Stellaluna* (Harcourt Brace & Co., 1993). This beautiful story of a bat raised by a bird emphasizes that despite their differences, the two creatures can still be friends.

Lester, Helen. *Tacky the Penguin* (Houghton Mifflin, 1990). Tacky likes to do things differently from the other penguins, but his unique behavior comes in handy when the hunters arrive with their traps.

Nikola-Lisa, W. *Bein' with You This Way* (Lee & Low Books, 1994). This catchy rap focuses positively on the differences among a multicultural group of people.

Celebrating Differences: Books to Share with Your Child

Ashley, Bernard. *Cleversticks* (New York: Crown Publishers, 1995). A young Asian boy feels like he can't do anything right at school—until he teaches his classmates how to use chopsticks.

Carlson, Nancy. *Arnie and the New Kid* (New York: Puffin Books, 1992). After he finds himself temporarily using crutches, Arnie learns to understand and be kinder to a classmate who uses a wheelchair.

Das, Prodeepta. *I is for INDIA* (Englewood Cliffs, NJ: Silver Burdett, 1996). An alphabet book that uses colorful photographs and descriptions to portray modern life in India.

Dorros, Arthur. *Abuela* (New York: Dutton, 1991). Rosalba and her grandmother *(abuela)* imagine themselves flying over New York City, enjoying the sights.

Fleming, Virginia. *Be Good to Eddie Lee* (New York: Philomel Books, 1993). A group of children learns to appreciate the talents of a boy with Down syndrome and to accept him as a friend.

Friedman, Ina R. *How My Parents Learned to Eat* (Boston: Houghton Mifflin, 1987). A little girl tells the story of how her parents met in Japan and learned about each other's cultures.

Hamanaka, Sheila. *All the Colors of the Earth* (New York: Morrow Junior Books, 1994). This book shows the spectrum of colors in nature and relates them to the skin tones of children.

Hoffman, Mary. *Amazing Grace* (Dial Books for Young Readers, 1991). With her grandmother's support and her own faith in herself, Grace overcomes barriers of race and gender discrimination to win a part in the school play.

Lester, Helen. *Tacky the Penguin* (Boston: Houghton Mifflin, 1990). Tacky likes to do things differently from the other penguins, but his unique behavior comes in handy when the hunters arrive with their traps.

Martin, Bill Jr., and John Archambault. *Knots on a Counting Rope* (New York: Henry Holt & Co., 1987). Challenged by blindness, a young Native American boy receives strength and encouragement from his grandfather, who tells him how special he is.

Nikola-Lisa, W. *Bein' with You This Way* (New York: Lee & Low Books, 1994). This catchy rap focuses positively on the differences among a multicultural group of people.

Ringgold, Faith. *Dinner at Aunt Connie's House* (New York: Hyperion Paperbacks for Children, 1996). Twelve famous African-American women step out of their portraits and tell a family about their courageous lives.

Simon, Norma. *Why Am I Different?* (Niles, IL: Albert Whitman, 1993). An exploration of the many kinds of differences among children, including the foods they eat, the homes in which they live, and the types of families to which they belong.

Waters, Kate, and Madeline Slovenz-Low. *Lion Dancer* (New York: Scholastic, 1990). New York City's Chinatown is the colorful setting for a young boy's debut as the Lion Dancer in the Chinese New Year's celebration.

About the Authors

Judy Lalli teaches second grade at Paul V. Fly School in Norristown, Pennsylvania, where she has taught for 26 years. She holds B.S. and M.S. degrees from the University of Pennsylvania, and she has completed extensive postgraduate work as well. As an adjunct professor for Wilkes University and Allentown College, Ms. Lalli teaches graduate education courses for teachers.

I Like Being Me—the book of poems on which this Leader's Guide is based—is Ms. Lalli's fourth book and her fourth collaboration with photographer Douglas L. Mason-Fry. Her earlier books include *Feelings Alphabet*, a celebration of 26 emotions portrayed through photographs and word graphics, and *Make Someone Smile and 40 More Ways to Be a Peaceful Person*, a book on peacemaking and conflict resolution for all ages.

Mary Martha Whitworth has been training teachers and child-care providers throughout the United States for over 25 years. She holds a B.A. degree from the University of Delaware and an M.A. degree from Marywood College, and has also completed extensive graduate work in the field of education. She has developed and currently teaches courses on self-esteem, communications skills, decision making and values, gender equity, conflict resolution, and curriculum enrichment using children's literature.

For ten years, Ms. Whitworth was the director of the Philadelphia Humanistic Education Center, where she created programs and trained consultants. As the owner of Skippack Children's Books, she won the prestigious national Pannell Award for her "Giving Tree" program. She is the coauthor of *Personalizing Education*, a handbook of educational strategies for teachers.

Just Because I Am: A Child's Book of Affirmation
by Lauren Murphy Payne, M.S.W., illustrated by Claudia Rohling

"I am a person. I am special. I am important . . . just because I am." Warm, simple words and enchanting illustrations strengthen and support young children's self-esteem.

For ages 3–8. 32 pp., color illust., s/c, 7⅝″ × 9¼″, ISBN 0-915793-60-1, $6.95

Leader's Guide. Thirteen lessons reinforce the messages of the child's book. Includes activities, questions, and reproducible Home Handouts for parents.

Preschool through grade 3. 56 pp., illust., s/c, 8½″ × 11″, ISBN 0-915793-61-X, $12.95

We Can Get Along: A Child's Book of Choices
by Lauren Murphy Payne, M.S.W., illustrated by Claudia Rohling

Simple words and inviting illustrations teach children how to get along with others and resolve conflicts peacefully.

For ages 3–8. 36 pp., color illust., s/c, 7⅝″ × 9¼″, ISBN 1-57542-013-9, $9.95

Leader's Guide. Fifteen lessons reinforce the messages of the child's book. Includes activities, questions, and reproducible Home Handouts for parents.

Preschool through grade 3. 64 pp., illust., s/c, 8½″ × 11″, ISBN 1-57542-014-7, $14.95

To place an order, or to request a free copy of our catalog, write or call:

Free Spirit Publishing, Inc.
400 First Avenue North, Suite 616
Minneapolis, MN 55401-1730
toll free (800) 735-7323, local (612) 338-2068
email: help4kids@freespirit.com